Triple Take
A Museum Story

Also by Robert Barclay

Non-fiction
> *The Art of the Trumpet-maker*
> *The Preservation and Use of Historic Musical Instruments*
> *Making a Natural Trumpet (with M. Münkwitz and R.*
> > *Seraphinoff)*
> *Henry VIII's Motorcycle: Or a Tale of Two Trumpets*

Fiction
> *Death at the Podium*
> *Ask Me About My Bombshells*
> *Jacob the Trumpeter*
> *His Majesty's Grand Conceit*
> *Conversations Between Sensible People*
> *Twixt Myth and History*

TRIPLE TAKE
A MUSEUM STORY

Robert Barclay

NATIONAL LIBRARY OF CANADA
CATALOGUING IN PUBLICATION DATA

Title: Triple take : a museum story / Robert Barclay.
Names: Barclay, R. L., author
Description: Third edition. | Previously published under pseudonym
Carl Eton.
Identifiers: Canadiana 2025012369X | ISBN 9781988657394
(softcover)
Subjects: LCGFT: Novels.
Classification: LCC PS8603.A7244 T75 2025 | DDC C813/.6—dc23

Copyright © 2025 Robert Barclay

Published by
LOOSE CANNON PRESS

loosecannonpress@gmail.com
www.loosecannonpress.com

ACKNOWLEDGEMENTS

M any museums have their dinosaurs on display in their public galleries; in this story, the museum's dinosaurs are ensconced in the curatorial, service, and administration offices. In order to craft an intricate and enjoyable plot, it was necessary to situate it in a dysfunctional institute. There's no fun in telling stories about well-run organizations filled with balanced and sensible people! So, it is necessary, first, to acknowledge the many wonderful and well-run museums and allied heritage institutions around the world that I have visited and worked with over a long career in the business of museum object conservation. My fictional institution—which could be anywhere, or nowhere, in the entire world—is the exception that proves the rule.

I must give a bow to the colleagues I have worked with over the years. Their intelligence, humour and wit made work into a joy and, most important, continually reinforced the light side of trying to get the job done within a bureaucracy that increasingly valued process over product. I am especially indebted to my colleague and friend Leslie Carlyle, whose novel *Masterpiece of Deception* (written under the pen name of Judy Lester), made me realize that perhaps I had a novel in me as well. I enjoyed bouncing ideas and bits of text off David Tremain and Cliff McCawley when the first edition was in draft, while my son David gave encouragement at every stage. Lena Samson kindly reviewed this third edition. My writing colleagues, too numerous to name individually, were always there. And where would any of my accomplishments be without my loving and supportive wife Janet? It remains to be seen what more she will let me get away with. Thank you, one and all, and please excuse the omissions.

Robert Barclay,
Ottawa 2025

AUTHOR'S NOTE

This novel is set in an imaginary island, almost a subcontinent. The human characters, the mythical beings, and all their interactions sprang entirely out of my head. I have taken these pains out of respect for all who dwell in the world in which you are reading this book. Any resemblance to real persons or beings, living or dead, is not intended, and the museum described here is entirely imaginary. The incidents, actions, locations and other aspects of the storyline are also fictitious.

SETTING THE SCENE

L ike all non-Western cultures exposed to colonization, the island nation in this story suffered friction between those who were already there, and those who came along later. The people of the latter were raised, educated, and inculcated with the assurance of cultural and political superiority, so when they occupied any new territory, it was with the manifest aim of pushing aside and sequestering the existing culture, and eventually absorbing it. Racial inferiority was a given, and thus education to the settlers' Western standards was applied with energy. An apartheid was established where isolation in designated locations was coupled with subsistence financing and forced educational integration.

Strangely, in spite of the colonizers' low opinion of the culture of the original people, their works of art were treasured and prized. There was a paradoxical relationship between reverence for the works of art and contempt for their creators. The process of collecting was an action of cultural encapsulation, and went hand in hand with assimilation; they were compiling a time capsule of the culture before they swept it away. They also harboured the assumption that depriving the owners of their ceremonial objects, by force if necessary, was in line with converting and re-educating them.

The embattled original people exhibited a strong resistance to assimilation and, although marginalized, maintained their cultural and craft practices wherever they could, often in secret. In solidarity, they came together and called themselves We Who Were Here First, which was soon shortened to WeWho. This naming caught on and became applied throughout the island. In time, their ceremonies and beliefs became respected, and some hegemony and self-government were granted. Nevertheless, they were a long way from being equal partners in the administration of their homeland, and perhaps never would be.

CHAPTER ONE

I t was a 'glittering soirée,' as arts reporters would gush the next morning. And it did so befit the occasion. It's not often that a museum collection marks its 75th anniversary, so now in the year 1985, the officials of the Museum of Personkind had decided to mark the event in style. The display gallery of the Treaty Bluff Collection— holding 98 exquisitely made pieces of the WeWho's wood carving— had been transformed into a reception hall for hundreds of guests, who were favoured with drinks, canapés, and a string quintet. Tides of partygoers washed around the display cases, glasses and little sausages on sticks in hand, as they viewed the great works of art and craft on display. Cunningly arranged spotlights threw their beams into the glass display cases, so that the artifacts occupied pools of light in a general penumbra. The effect was rich and luxurious.

Strolling between display cases and among the swirling, tinkling, and chattering guests was Bill Anker, the director of the museum. He was just a very ordinary museum director; a short, bald, bespect-acled, ineffectual looking man of middle age. No one present could have mistaken him for a man of influence. On his arm, and virtually welded there, was Doris his wife. Here was a contrast! She was a stern, tough-faced woman of medium height, 35 or so years old with light brown hair and clear grey eyes, and undoubtedly imbued with an iron will. She was of the Naval Ironsides, who sit at the right hand of God.

The cut of Doris's jib was hardly romantic, and her family back-ground precluded open displays of sentimentality. On the face of it, their alliance seemed quite unlikely. But she had met him in peculiar circumstances at a diplomatic reception when he was just a junior curator, and some strange alchemy had done the rest. Bill Anker was her life's project; it was only through her constant monitoring over all their years that this unlikely clay had been formed into the dubious shape of a museum director. One had to know people.

In the early years of the 20th century the ethnologists from the State Museum of Man (as it was then known) had assembled a collection second to none in quality and meaning. Everything they collected on their methodical sweep through the nation was brought to a central repository in the middle of the country, near a place called Treaty Bluff, before the planned shipping to the capital city for safe-keeping, preservation, study and display.

But a Great War intervened, and the collectors' attention became focused upon the place from which they had originated, on horrors they should have left behind. The chief ethnologist died a captain in a stinking trench; one of many heroes and fools to fill graves in a foreign land. The collection languished. Ironically, the indigenous people of Treaty Bluff became the interim custodians of the material.

It was only in the 1920s that the collection finally came to its present resting place in the State Museum of Man. The Treaty Bluff Collection, as it came to be known, became the hub of the museum's holdings. Over the years, other artifacts of historical, folk culture, and archaeological interest were added to fill out the human story. But this core remained the finest and the best.

As Bill and Doris absorbed the cultural scenery and mingled with the mob, the couple were spotted by the museum's chief of conservation, who began to make his way in their direction.

'Oh, Christ!' muttered Doris. 'It's that evil bastard Easel. Can't we escape?'

'Too late,' murmured her husband as the creature elbowed his way in their direction.

Woodrow Wilson Easel was a muscular, hard-faced man of 40 or so, with short, curly hair and strangely disturbing eyes. Although he was the chief of just one of the many departments, Easel ran the museum. It's that simple. People just did as they were told. He was a frightener and a manipulator, and it was far simpler to do as he wished just to make him go away. He wasn't going away at the moment.

'Nice lil swah-ray we got goin' here,' observed Easel, staring directly at Anker and then giving his wife a lascivious up-and-down sweep of the eyes. 'Always nice t' cast y'r eyes over beautifully made works of art, eh?'

Anker quailed. Easel never failed to allude to a horrible secret they shared; an unspeakable truth about this entire collection that would mean Anker's ruin and the museum's embarrassment. This was Easel's control card, and he used it often and well.

'Yes, yes, very fine indeed!' replied Anker, keeping his voice as level as he was able. 'Always nice to give the museum some publicity. Ha, ha.'

'Yeah, publicity's just great, isn't it? Jus' what's needed. Specially *this* collection.' And he wheeled away.

3

'What the hell's he getting at?' asked Doris. 'That bugger never says anything without sounding threatening, or snide, or... or... something! And he can't even speak proper English! Why haven't you got rid of him?'

'Get rid of him? *You* try!'

'I loathe him. He's evil. And you should do something about him.'

Bill Anker stuck his nose into his drink. This was an oft-repeated conversation and it never went anywhere. He spotted John Indoda Enhle, the chief executive of the WeWho Arts Council, peering closely at a wooden mask, and he extricated himself from Doris's arm, leaving her to corner the chairperson of the Board of Trustees.

John Indoda Enhle had a wide face with an aquiline nose, clear brown eyes flecked with amber, and the dark olive skin and black hair of the people who had lived on this land long before Anker's lot had shown up.

When Anker saw *which* mask Indoda Enhle was examining so closely, he realized his mistake in joining him. Oh, my God! he thought. Not another of my horrible secrets! He made to turn but it was too late; Indoda Enhle had seen him.

Indoda Enhle knew a great deal more about this collection than the museum gave him credit for. How many of the curators, he wondered, know that I was born and raised in Treaty Bluff? Boy, what they would give for my knowledge! But I don't know if they care that much. He'd had a stint on the museum's board of trustees some years ago, but hadn't made much of an impression. Hell, his invitation to this little shindig had only happened the day before; he suspected they had only remembered their manners at the last minute, in one of those oh-shit moments. Anyway, here he was with a glass in hand, and a secret hoard of information that, frankly, he wished he wasn't privy to.

'Do you know this little fellah's story?' he asked, indicating the mask in the display case with his thumb.

Do I? Oh, Jesus, do I? thought Anker, his terror threatening to expose itself.

'N-no,' he lied. 'My graduate degree was in social history, not ethnology.' *Please, please, don't dig too deep!*

Yeah, thought Indoda Enhle, social history's what happens to you guys; ethnology is what happens to the rest of us. Things *have* to change.

'His name is N'ufnīvah, the Hare. He's the joker, the trickster

4

among the people of the lakes and woods. It's his job to throw discord into people's lives. Did you know that?'

My God, he couldn't be more appropriate, could he? thought Anker.

'No, no, I didn't, but I hope he doesn't try anything here! Ha, ha...' Knowing in his heart that he already had.

'No chance of that. I think you've got him quite tamed.' He turned away to refresh his glass. 'But keep an eye on him, won't you?'

Anker's terror began to subside as attention on the mask receded. But a third party intruded, and all his fears came howling back, almost unmasking him. Rourke Mutcer (pronounced moot-zehr, more or less), was Anker's chief curator and effectively second-in-command. He was a tall, well-built man who dressed carefully, was very conscious of his appearance, and could lay on the charm. He lusted after Bill Anker's job, he was privy to his horrible secret, and he knew that one day he would be able to use it to his advantage. N'ufnīvah the Hare had played some wicked tricks already.

'Oh, yes, the Hare,' he chipped in, having caught most of the conversation. 'He really does play wicked tricks, doesn't he Bill?'

Indoda Enhle turned back. Mutcer stared hard at Anker. Anker tried, and failed, to return the stare. His terror *must* be showing. He was sweating and his heartrate was rocketing.

'What sort of wicked tricks are you thinking of?' asked Indoda Enhle, wondering if these people knew what he knew.

'Oh, nothing really,' temporized Mutcer, wishing only to terrorize Anker, not expose him. 'Just some problems with conservation treatment, materials analysis, that sort of thing. Technical stuff really.'

Indoda Enhle turned away again in some relief and sought the drinks and canapés.

'Whew!' said Mutcer, pretending to loosen his tie. 'Do you find it hot in here? Know what I mean?'

Mutcer continued to eye Anker until, shamed and powerless, his director turned away.

At moments like this he hated being director even more than usual, although he never *really* enjoyed it. It was only because of Doris... But make no mistake, Bill Anker loved the museum and all it stood for—culture, artisanship, the tantalizing glimpses of the past, the beguiling search for historical verities—but he just wished he was still a lowly curator with none of the cares of office heaped upon him.

He escaped a grinning Mutcer, and ran metaphorically into the arms of Doris, who was conversing with the minister of culture and professional sport. (Amateur sport as a concept worth supporting had died out some years before.) The minister was one of those annoying people who will keep saying 'going forward,' as if time had the option of flowing backwards or even sideways.

The Ironsides moved in high ministerial social circles, and the minister was well acquainted with Doris's father, the Admiral, who had parlayed family money into a very considerable real estate empire. Admiral Ironside had access to an obscenely large amount of ready money, and the minister knew it.

It was a supreme feat of will that made Bill Anker transform himself from an abject figure of terror and misery into a consort fit for Doris Ironside-Anker, and it is a testament to some fortitude in him that he accomplished it. By the time he hove alongside he was calm and composed, and could join in the social chit-chat with some aplomb. He just hated occasions like this, and hoped there wouldn't be many more. What in God's name would the 100th anniversary be like? Thank God he wouldn't be here to see it.

And the 100th would most certainly be celebrated in style. One thing about this museum's funding: there was always sufficient money for food, drink, and entertainment for the upper crust. The Museum of Personkind was an agency that had benefited from a cultural policy that laid down the maxim that if there was a problem, money should be shoved at it in sufficient quantities to shut it up, and no more. Money had been flung in limited showers since the government of the day had woken to the fact that culture, in a manipulable form, can buy votes. Lovely museums filled with priceless treasures are Culture made concrete.

Defining culture is among the most difficult tasks in the English language, which is why it is so open to kidnap and ransom by those who have little grasp on its many meanings. The present government was a mean-minded oligarchy whose members were not, themselves, 'cultured.' It was said that the cultures within the lower bowels of the museum board members showed more variety and richness than any apprehended by their sense organs. But they still funded fine museums, and the comestibles that made the wheels run smoothly. Just a pity, thought Bill, that the cash for champagne and paté, crackers, and those little sausages on sticks, couldn't be spent on care of collections... or a new building.

So, the glittering soirée trundled along; the string quintet scrubbed away at Schubert, museum staff and honoured guests gazed into *vitrines*, consumed their wines and cheeses and little bits of *paté* on crackers, and held forth on the beauty of the *objets d'art*, and the skill of their *artisans*. Every member of this social elite drifted in a sea of contentment and privilege. You could tell how classy the event was by the number of French words needed to describe it.

Things were different outside the gallery. In the adjoining hall stood Lucian Limace, the sweaty, corpulent chief of security. It was his job to ensure that all went smoothly on occasions like this. He'd already had his hands full with the press, who were keen to file reports for their social columns. A change from break-and-enters anyway, thought Limace. He would have liked to delegate the job to one of his underlings—he was giftedly lazy and loathed any social occasion—but duty demanded he be there. Jee-zus! The Security Department *had* to show some presence, with all these stuffed up shirt-'n'-ties and whatnot around, God damn it.

But what was this? A goddam intruder! Some skinny, mean-mouthed woman was coming down the corridor towards him. The front security downstairs should have stopped her. Shit! Do I have to do everybody's goddam job?

'Eh! Ow did you get in? On'y museum staff and guests in here!' croaked Limace, bummed out at having to assert his authority when he should have been at home watching the game on the box and drinking beer.

'Just wanna see what's goin' on, that's all,' answered the woman, peeping through the glass doors into the gallery. She carried a notepad and pen, and had bull-shitted her way in by claiming to be a reporter. She eyed the party-goers jealously.

Sue Tortfeasor (or Tort for short, all the way through high school and beyond) was a professional protester, and had been for years. Her gene for righteous sense of indignation was dominant, and it didn't take much for her to get on the old high horse. Hearing of this gathering on the radio, and now peering in the doors at the stuffing, swilling multitude living off the stolen artistic legacy of a subjugated people really pissed her off.

'I gotta do something about this,' she thought, although what she would or could do was still ill-formed in her mind.

Before Limace's moist paw plopped onto her shoulder and spun her round, she glimpsed John Indoda Enhle among the crowd. She'd heard of him, and suspected he could be some kind of lever, provide some kind of access, be somewhat sympathetic, something…

'Aw right! Out! Out!'

She left the scene reluctantly with thoughts of mayhem on her mind.

CHAPTER TWO

A carpenter from the wooden artifacts lab had been summoned to the office of the museum's chief of conservation in Building Four, some distance from the main museum. And summoned was the right word. His career in the Museum of Personkind looked to be taking one hell of a downturn, if recent events were anything to go by. He was a thin, wiry guy all sinew and not an ounce of fat, with deft, easy movements and short, cropped hair. He looked like a triathlete, and probably was. He stepped into the office and closed the door behind him. His chief, Woodrow Wilson Easel, studiously ignored him and pretended to read a report bound in an elaborate folder.

'You wanted to see me?' No response. Not a flicker of the eyes. The report reading continued.

The Carpenter stood and waited. Nothing. This was typical; the usual head game to get him off guard. Okay, screw you, play along. We've been here before. He remained at attention.

His mind roved over the last few years. He'd had no training for the job of conservation, having never studied science and all that stuff, but he loved wood and woodworking tools. He knew what to do when working on historic things, he loved to read about history, and he was very careful and methodical. He had started his career in the museum workshop as a carpenter. He was one of those who have the hands and the eyes and the brain, and all the magical neural interconnections in between, that make them the fixers, the creators, the improvisers. The people who make materials jump through hoops.

But even though he worked in the conservation lab, he was still classified as a carpenter. You needed paper qualifications to be a conservator these days, and a kinder hierarchy would have helped him get further training and development. Such career advancement would have been unlikely on Easel's watch anyway, and now it would never happen because he had got on the wrong side of the bastard. He hadn't meant to. Not really. There were two incidents.

In the first one, a loan exhibition of jewelry and fine sculpture entitled *Gold and Gems* was being installed. Easel was there, overseeing some conservation-related issue regarding the installation. While giving his advice he had picked up a solid gold statuette by the Japanese sculptor Etsugua Nidor with his bare hands. Now, it is a museum rule that white cotton gloves be used at all times when handling objects. To see the chief of conservation ignoring such a fundamental policy was a temptation just too good to let go. The Carpenter wished he had stayed in the background and not got himself involved. But he hadn't. He had quietly walked forward and wordlessly proffered a pair of spotless white gloves. The expression on the asshole's face had been frightening.

From that day forward the chief of conservation made things miserable for him. Not content with continual criticism of his woodworking, he had started on a campaign of lies. The Carpenter would hear nasty little tales about himself, and trace them back to their source in his chief. He could have fought. Maybe he should have. He would have loved to punch the bastard's face in.

And then there was the second incident, which was probably why he was standing here now. He had needed the chief of conservation's signature on an overtime form, and had walked into Easel's office without knocking. The door had been left slightly ajar.

What he saw was Easel standing on his chair and lifting a fairly large file box into an aperture in the ceiling where a tile had been pushed aside. The ceiling tiles were suspended on wires from the beams, and there was a considerable space above hung with pipes, conduits and cables. On hearing him enter Easel had reacted like a cornered raccoon and literally hissed the Carpenter out of the office. There were rumors that his boss kept secret files on everybody in the museum, and here was some great corroboration.

Now, here he was standing in front of the boss, with those eyes mercifully boring into a document and not him, and wondering what sort of punitive action was going to be taken. Eventually, having stretched contempt as far as he judged necessary, Easel raised his head slowly from his document and fixed the young man with eyes filled with distain. He was enjoying punishing the employee standing there in front of him, and he let it show. He was one of those people who have the horrible gift of showing hatred solely through the magnetism of their eyes.

Once fixed on him, the stare never left the Carpenter's face. 'Jus' to tell you to clear your stuff out and get lost. Human Resources've got all the papers.'

Just like that! At first, he was speechless, then it began to register. 'You can't... you can't just...'

'Oh, yes, I can! You bin on contracts. I can choose to terminate a contract whenever I like. It's discredible conduct. There's all kinds of incidences.'

'You... you... bastard! I'll...'

'You'll what?'

'You... you'll see. I'll get you. You'll see,' he stammered. Easel fixed him with the stare again. He felt all his energy leave him.

'Just try it, sonny. You wanna drop the gloves with me? Just try it! Now get out.'

The Carpenter walked down the corridor to the front door in a daze, carrying a small tool pouch and some few papers he had grabbed out of his desk. By the time he had walked halfway to Human Resources in the main building to get his papers sorted out, his shock had turned into a blazing fury. He wanted to kick and smash and destroy. He knew what sick hatred Easel could generate, but he had no idea of how suddenly he would act. Out of a job! Just like that. Son of a bitch!

He entered the main museum building and sprinted up the stairs to the fifth floor, avoiding the slow, ancient elevator. He hated to go up there, but there would be no pay cheque if he didn't. Still, it hurt like hell. He finished the business as soon as possible, still seething, and turned towards the elevator. As he passed the front reception, he saw that the receptionist had left a small purse unattended on the desk. In a cold and calculating gesture he picked it up, stuffed it in his pocket, and exited quickly down the stairs.

Normally he would take the bus home, but today he walked, trying to calm himself. As his anger subsided and a stratum of depression set in, he began to feel guilty over the theft of the purse. That was mean. A sudden gesture of defiance at the museum, but some innocent person would suffer. He would have to find some way of giving it back.

As he walked, things got shaken more into perspective. He was down by the river, on one of the bike paths that threaded the town. It was early in November, cold but clear, and the freshness did a lot for his head. A wind whipped off the chilled water. Dried tears streaked one cheek. This wasn't the end. He was still relatively young—only a little over 30—and there was lots of opportunity in this town. But the museum was so right for him. So right!

And there was Stephanie, too. He really thought things were going well there, but she had suddenly gone cold and distant. As if losing your job wasn't enough! What to do now? Look for work, I suppose.

As he walked, the blackness threatening him started slowly to recede. Gradually a plan began to form in his mind. Vengeance may be ugly, but in this case it was more than justified. No, he wouldn't give the purse back just yet. In fact, from now on, other things would start to go missing. Seeing his ex-boss handling that gold statuette and sticking that box into the ceiling had given him an idea...

The museum that had kicked a valuable staff member into the street without ceremony was not new to thoughtless dealings with fellow human beings.

At its foundation in the early years of the century the mandate of the State Museum of Man was the collection, study and preservation of examples of the arts and crafts of primitive cultures. This included all the original people who were being pushed out of the way by the steam locomotive, the multi-bottomed plough, and the priests. The motives of these white civilizers from across the ocean were beyond reproach, but *only* if understood in the context of their own times. And this is something that requires more an act of faith than a reading of history. And no amount of retrospective historical perfume can expunge the stink of cultural imperialism from a nation's nostrils.

Victorian civilization, hard work and faith in their God lay at the root of their being. Evolution, progress and development were powerful sources of motive power, still fresh and bright from their minting in an industrial ethos. These people sincerely believed it to be their appointed task to raise up the poor native wherever in the world they found him; to bring him to God and to labour and to the English tongue, and to his just reward in heaven. They were driven by steam and sanctity.

Hard on the heels of the mechanizers, settlers, wheeler-dealers, sharks, whores, and Jesus-salesmen came the ethnologists and the anthropologists; the museum people. It was their job to scoop up, enshrine and preserve time capsules of the cultures that were fast being subsumed. They collected, catalogued and systematized in that positivistic way that believes everything to be subject to order and method. The march of History herself was both a proselytizing tool and a predictive science. The savants from the State Museum of Man scoured the plains, the forests, and the mountains.

It is difficult to understand from a 21st century perspective how the good intentions of these white men from across the sea could be reconciled with their laws and their behaviour. How could it be, for example, that to execute bold, expressive and highly skilled carving in wood could be made illegal? But it was. An act of parliament proscribed the carving of cultural emblems of any sort, and subjected its practitioners to prison sentences.

Of course, they carved anyway. The WeWho knew exactly where the police could put their laws. None of their ceremonies, none of their traditional education and lore, and none of their language was permitted. So, wherever the police or the priests had banned the dancers and confiscated their regalia, the curators were ready with their straw, and packing crates and shipping labels.

So it was that the Treaty Bluff collection arrived at the museum from its temporary holding place. When it left Treaty Bluff its local custodians seemed surprisingly glad to be rid of it, and showed no reluctance in speeding it on its way. Quite the reverse; they organized a joyous celebration of dancing, drumming and singing while the crates and boxes were loaded onto the train. This attitude ought to have provoked some thought among the curators and ethnologists, but in those days, although they studied the original people intensively, it was as specimens rather than as human beings in possession of freewill, philosophic thought and humour.

Especially humour.

CHAPTER THREE

It was a Monday, now late in November, and it had snowed a great deal already. Bill Anker, was staring distractedly down from the window of his fifth-floor office in the main museum building. A thin sleet swirled around the traffic in the street below, lit and coloured by streetlights and traffic signals, and people walked quickly with shoulders hunched. The scene matched his mood.

He mused upon how he had got to where he was now. He had to be honest with himself; he knew that the real world, outside the museum's walls, would not have been kind to him. He had no marketable skills really. But here, safe inside, he was comfortable among other similarly afflicted souls.

Had he been running a financial institution he would probably have brought it to its knees on the exchanges of the world in a week. Had he been an artist, or designer, or poet he would have starved in a month. Had he been... anything... he would surely have been a miserable and unremembered failure, struggling from hand-to-mouth in a pitiless world that takes no heed of the ones who just don't quite have it. Museum administration was his lifeboat. For Anker, as for many like him, the museum was a haven; a warm, welcoming anchorage where he could float among his own kind.

Anker appeared to have worked his way up the hierarchy of his home museum not by application, but by attrition. Through some bizarre chemistry there never seemed to be a better person for a promotion when one came around. Bill Anker was always there, obtrusive, and chosen for advancement not because of his skills, but because a hole existed and he was always second best in a field that had no better. Promotion in the museum was like deficit budgeting; it isn't what you've got so much as what you haven't got. Anker hadn't got much, but his colleagues had even less of what he hadn't got. And so he got on. And he appeared successful.

There was also a great deal of help from the wings, but he was never really sure of how much. He would have been humiliated to know the true extent of the Ironside arm-twisting in high places.

There is a niche in society for everybody, no matter how disadvantaged, and it is the lifelong quest of most people to find that niche, and to settle into it for the duration. The prime role of Anker's museum was not the one expressed in its brand-new mission statement: the safeguarding of cultural heritage and the display of the Nation's social wealth. No. Quite simply, its role was to supply one of those niches. And it was a large one.

The director turned from the wintry scene outside his window and surveyed his office. He had filled his workspace with assemble-it-yourself Swedish furniture. This, at least, he was quite proud of. It had all come in heavy boxes with names like Dikk and Bålux. It was hard to assemble, but the display technicians with their little wrenches had helped a lot. He rose to his full height behind his Dümklük executive walnut veneer desk (five feet six inches in the shoes Doris had bought him at that special store, because he couldn't bring himself to go in there). He polished his half-moon glasses distractedly on the wide end of his tie.

His baldness irked him, although he knew it shouldn't. Well, bald men do look intellectual; all that vast expanse of dynamic cranium exposed to view. No, it was the shine. Why was his head so damned glossy? He looked at his hands. A perfect matte finish, like the finest acrylic varnish. Nowhere on his whole body was shiny except his head. Why? He knew it wasn't just his imagination; he had seen scintillations of it reflected in his colleagues' glasses on many occasions. He was always careful where he sat during slide presentations.

He sighed as he thought of these things, and plumped himself down wearily in his five-wheeled swivel chair. While in his office, Anker took to lighting his face from below by a cunningly angled desk lamp. His staff wondered why he wished to appear ghoulish, because when he looked up from his work it was with the expression of a startled grave robber. Now, as he sat behind his desk, his bald eminence became lost in shadow and his face hung above his three-piece suit like a flabby and deflated autumn moon.

The Ankers were of Norwegian stock. Family legend had a famous Oslo governor roosting firmly in some branch of the family tree. Bill just wished some of those legendary Viking attributes had come down to him. He imagined his immediate ancestors carving out a place for themselves with axes in the island's woodlands, just as their early forebears had landed in wooden ships and carved their way through remote Northumbrian monasteries. He pictured them as tall, thickly blonde, muscled and ruthless. Were there, he wondered, short and plump, not very assertive, near-sighted, bald ones as well? Oh, dear…

But, my God, what a Monday! More sleet rattled against the windows. It had been an awful day. One stupid thing after another. There had been a series of mysterious petty thefts going back about three weeks—mostly small, personal things belonging to staff—and another had been brought to his attention today. So that took half the morning while the owner was mollified and a report filed.

And now, the news he had just received made the petty thefts seem insignificant: they had turned down the funding for the new building! After years of scheming and planning, committee meeting after committee meeting, and acres of architect's drawings, the minister was not going to support his proposal. It was impossible. God damn their funding of pop concerts in the park and crappy outdoor sculptures made by morons, when museums were falling to bits!

And the truly shitty thing was, they had announced their decision in a cheap, cowardly e-mail circulated to all committee members. Didn't even have the balls to call him first, or even talk to him! This news put a damper on any reward the job might still have to offer.

In a way it had been his own fault. He admitted this, but only to himself. In an effort to justify the new building, he had initiated a survey of the present accommodations with a view to establishing their inferiority. Had he chosen to employ an external consultant the inadequacies of the facilities would have become readily apparent. But with his typical organizational myopia he had had the job done by his own conservation staff, and the fools had reported that things were just fine! A thick binder of 252 pages of exhaustive survey of accommodations and physical plant in four buildings, all to say that everything was fine, thank you very much! Stupid buggers! And of course, when the report was finished, they very efficiently fired off copies to everybody. Impossible to retract.

When they see a museum, most people assume that it's all under one roof. The building *is* the museum. This is almost never the case. The four buildings that Anker's staff had surveyed is about the average for a large museum. Collections accumulate over the years, and planners, architects and financiers never manage to keep up. The needs outstrip the facilities in a continuous and self-perpetuating game of catch-up. So, the Museum of Personkind had expanded over the years to occupy four buildings, one in a neighbourhood fairly remote from the main display building. None of the buildings had been designed as a museum. Initially, all were grossly substandard.

The main exhibition building, from which Anker disconsolately surveyed the street below, was a Neo-Classical ex-department store with 'fading delusions of grandeur,' as the architectural wonks would say. The collections were moved in a hurry to this bankrupt building in the 1940s when the original museum was destroyed by a sudden subsidence due to erosion of the riverbank. This temporary accommodation proved to be permanent. It was the building that bore most of the external beautifying because it was the facade the public saw, and it had been accorded a heritage designation. It was located in the centre of town only a short distance from the Parliament. Its grand facade was fronted by eight Corinthian columns, surmounted by a triangular entablature in the Classical tradition. A flight of fine wide steps led up to big oaken front doors.

Behind the facade and through these doors the building was divided into five floors, reminiscent of its original layout as a department store. A central foyer, all five storeys in height and surrounded by balconies, ran from front to back of the building. The stairs to the upper floors were at the rear of the foyer and ascended left and right. To the left as one entered the front doors—the east side of the building—was the Treaty Bluff collection; the artifacts of the original people collected at the beginning of the century. They occupied the second and third floors. The first floor on this side was divided in half: the front part was occupied by a number of historical dioramas, and at the rear were a couple of small offices and the loading bay, which opened onto the rear parking lot. The fourth floor had the ballroom for museum social functions, and a lecture theatre. Finally, on the fifth floor were storage facilities and mechanical rooms for the building environmental control. On the west side—to the right as one came through the doors—were the gift shop and cafeteria, and on the second and third floors the more recently acquired displays of history, folk culture and archaeology. The fourth and fifth floors were divided into offices for much of the museum curatorial staff, including the director.

The museum was closed on Mondays. This was a tradition that arose when it was necessary to close the galleries for routine maintenance, cleaning, changing of the displays, and so on. Over the years there was less and less need to do anything in the public areas of the museum but the tradition persisted, and staff's routines were arranged around it.

Earlier that afternoon, just before Bill Anker had learned of the death of his new museum hopes, a security guard walked through the temporary exhibition *Gold and Gems* three floors below. He was a fairly young man, and quite new to the job. It wasn't what he wanted to be doing—he was good with electronics and machinery—but it was easy, it paid the rent, and it was a short breather after he had been laid off from his previous job. He had worked as a technician for a firm that made and tested security equipment, and he looked with irony at the present boom in such equipment, and compared it with a firm that had gone bust only months before. This job had been suggested by a carpenter friend of his who just been booted out of the conservation department. Well, it was a stopgap, and it was in security, even if he was grossly over-qualified.

In fact, the job would be just fine for the time being if it wasn't for the boss, the slug-chief of Museum Security. He'd had bad bosses before, but never one like this! This one was a real beauty, but at least he didn't come across him very often. Ah, things could be worse, and it was only until something better came up. But now he had a task that had nothing to do with museum security. Quite the reverse, in fact.

The guard wasn't paying much attention to the fabulous wealth and glittering beauty on display behind the glass panels, until he came to the case containing the golden statuette by the Japanese sculptor Etsugua Nidor. Even then he was not interested in the work of art, so much as the security fittings of the display case. He was sweating buckets and glancing around nervously even though, being Monday, the museum was closed and deserted. And he had switched off the closed-circuit security cameras. Removing a screwdriver with a specially shaped head from his pocket he quickly loosened two of the four screws that held the glass top in place, dropping them casually on the floor at his feet.

He continued on his rounds, checking doors and turning light switches until he reached the security booth beside the front door. He placed the screwdriver safely in a desk drawer, flipped the random scanning security cameras back on, and fiddled a bit with their programming. He then picked up the phone and called the Conservation Department in Building Four.

'Museum security. There's some screws loose in the display. That gold Japanese thing in *Gold and Gems*. Yeah, I just seen it.'

Building Four was three blocks south, a 10-minute walk from

the main museum building, across two busy intersections. It had been a sausage factory in its heyday, and it was many years after the museum's occupation that generations of voracious rats could be finally persuaded that no further delicious scraps were forthcoming. The building was almost square in plan, with a fairly high ceiling, and was internally divided to make a complex of labs and storage facilities. This building had had a great deal of energy and money spent on it because here were stored some of the finest specimens, about which this story begins to revolve.

Old and delicate objects made of wood and other organic materials require a high degree of environmental control, so storage rooms had been tailor-made for them. The extensive labs of the Conservation Department were situated in this building as well because the restoration, cleaning, and repair of objects and works of art also requires excellent heating and ventilating facilities and efficient fume extraction systems. The labs of the Archaeology Department, where specimens were cleaned and prepared, shared some of the space.

Woodrow Wilson Easel was pissed off, but it never took much. Screws loose? Yeah, right! None of his staff worked on Monday afternoons; it was the agreed-upon flexible half-day as the museum was closed, and people made up for it on Saturday mornings.

So here was a stupid errand he would probably have to do himself. He put the guard on hold and dialed senior conservator Stephanie Chang's extension in the lab. Getting no answer, he poked his head out of his office and saw that her coat was gone from the rack near the door. Shit!

He almost regretted the day display case design and security had been brought under the Conservation Department's control. But it was one small part of the network of power and influence he had built up over the years, and he would hardly relinquish it now, pain in the ass though it was. The more fingers he had in other people's pies the better.

He picked up the phone again. 'All right, I'll be there in 10 minutes. Doan touch anythin'.'

He collected the special display case security screwdriver and headed over to the museum. He didn't bother to sign in at the front door, although he was supposed to as it was after hours. Security was lax, and everybody knew him anyway. With hardly a nod to the security guard he quickly ascended the stairs and entered the temporary exhibition area where *Gold and Gems* was set up. Sure enough, when he got to the gold statuette's display case, he found that two screws had been removed and dropped on the carpet. This was mighty fuckin' suspicious; galleries closed, nobody around, just that security loafer. What was going on here? He returned the screws to their correct places, giving each a vicious little extra twist.

When he got back down to the front door he leaned into the security booth. 'You jus' found 'em like that, eh?'

'Yeah, right there. Just as I was going through.'

'Jus' lyin' there, eh? What the fuck's going on here?'

'I dunno. I only know that's what I found.'

'Well, I find this goddam suspicious, lemme tell you!' He stared hard at the guard. There was something about his eyes... 'Aren't you friends with that carpenter? One of his buddies?'

'Yeah, he's okay. I like...'

'You choose your pals poorly mister. I threw him out. Just watch yourself, thass all.'

The security guard was fearful at the best of times of this creature Easel—the man who had spread poison about his best friend and then sacked him—and the thought of brazenly lying to him was agonizing. He could almost feel the man's suspicion, and if he ever discovered he had been deceived it would be curtains. Maintaining his composure was almost as much as he could bear. He was trembling and sweating, and it was obviously visible.

But Easel had this effect on people all the time; he enjoyed their discomfort, and it never occurred to him that the reaction he was seeing might have a reason other than his mere presence.

He stared for 10 seconds longer, appeared to shelve his suspicions, said 'All right,' gracelessly and left the building without another word. This needed a lot more thinking about...

His visit was omitted from the security logbook because he hadn't signed in, but a closed-circuit security video camera in the display area had caught him briefly.

The guard breathed a huge sigh of relief as he saw him go. That was just about the hardest thing he had ever been asked to do, and he was amazed with himself that he had pulled it off. He was neither a courageous nor an imaginative man, and a face-to-face confrontation with a person who had clearly taken a hate to him was hard to take. But he had done it!

He just hoped it was worthwhile, and wished he had never got sucked into all this. 'All this' was a series of petty thefts that had afflicted the museum for the last few weeks. Ever since his carpenter friend had been sacked, as a matter of fact.

His shift ended at 9:00 this evening, but before then he was expecting his friend to show up. This was the evening that the solid gold Japanese statuette was going to disappear! Oh, Christ! He was filled with fear all over again. Why did I agree to this?

Unknown to him, though, his peace was going to be mightily disturbed in the next hour or so, long before the Carpenter showed up. He would almost forget the role he would have to play this evening, but not quite.

Bill Anker wandered around his office on that dull, depressing, sleety Monday beating himself up for initiating the review of the buildings. He knew that somehow, by some means, he must find a way to twist a few influential arms. A new building really was not an option; it was a *necessity*.

The phone blasted him from his reverie, and he seized it jerkily.

'Well, of course it's urgent! People have been shunting up and down the stairs for days!'

The ancient bronze-grilled and ceramic-switched elevator was out of action again.

'Yes, they *are* complaining! Every damned day I get visitor complaints from people who had to use the stairs. That's what we provide Museum Feedback Sheets for. What? No, I don't give a damn if the exercise is good for them. Look, the director should not have to spend his time on such trivialities. Just get on to it, and get it fixed!'

He hung up. What was so hard about getting a contractor to service an elevator, for God's sake? He had more important things to deal with.

Back to the new museum. The government had to be convinced that nothing short of a brand-new building was possible. He would go to any lengths to achieve this goal. Not that his lengths were all that extensive.

Fundraising and political clout were really tasks for the Board of Trustees, of course. But the Board of the Museum of Personkind occupied a peculiar situation. Its constitution was theoretically vested with enormous power but, like British Royalty and Governors General,

21

used it infrequently and almost deferentially. The day-to-day running of the museum was of no concern to the members at all, and provided no adverse public waves were made, they interfered little, if at all. In times of great crisis, the Board might be obliged to wield its power, but the situation would need to be very grave indeed.

Quite simply, the Board's function in peaceful and unperturbed times, was to meet as frequently as necessary or possible, in luxurious surroundings (a boardroom on the fourth floor) so that retired paper mill chairmen and arts mavens could crumble little Swiss pastries and slurp fine coffee, or wine and perhaps liqueurs as the occasion and time of day demanded, and talk culture and politics and art. There were seven of them; a number chosen deliberately so that, should there ever be the need to vote on anything, there wouldn't be that sporting chance of a hung jury, such a terrible bore. The Chairperson, Mrs Straw, a well-meaning and well-connected lady of considerable girth, had managed to winkle her way into a prime position of influence by always taking the road which led to provision of the most edible and drinkable materials for the greatest number of mouths.

Such boards are usually composed of people with influence in the community, together with some vested interest in the object of their duties. In the modern parlance they are stakeholders. However, people with views and opinions and ideas make awkward table companions. By a process of natural selection, those members who actually had ideas upon the running of the museum, or visions of its direction and future, were gradually weeded out.

A torpor had settled over the Board; a boozy, replete indolence that gave the impression of the Roman court of Heliogabalus in a painting by Lawrence Alma-Tadema. This otiose lifestyle really ought to have gone on forever, but in this cold, late fall of the year there would be alarums aplenty to roust the members of the Board from their post-prandial stupors.

Anker knew the way money raising was done these days was with matching funds; museums were more and more frequently knocking on the doors of the private sector for big chunks of money, tied to all sorts of commercial considerations, with which to salt the public pot. The trouble was, it would take an organization or an individual with a large amount of money; an almost obscenely large amount of money. He picked up the phone and began making a series of calls to as many people of influence as he could think of. Not that many, unfortunately. The trouble was, he didn't really know anybody, and the few he was acquainted with hardly took him seriously.

Perhaps luckily for him—if only he had the gift of seeing away into the future—there was another, far more energetic and ruthless, who also had similar aspirations.

CHAPTER FOUR

Visitors entering a museum gallery fully expect to encounter 'the real thing.' That's what a museum visit is for. People raised in the Western tradition are searching for an authentic experience. But, because materials are fragile and evanescent, in many non-Western cultures the actual solid reality of the thing is not as important. If wood rots and leather decays and basketry falls apart, let it go. It's enough to make another with all the attributes, tangible and intangible, of the first. Not so in the West. The one copied from the original is a fake, a repro; a concept quite alien outside that materialistic, mercantile and acquisitive industrial ethos. So exhibiting copies instead of the originals is a cruel trick to put over on the museum visitors. It's a con. But, surely, if their experience on viewing these purported artistic treasures is indistinguishable from that of seeing the real thing, how does it matter?

Reproductions was the most richly endowed and heavily staffed department in the Museum of Personkind. In its labs in Building Three were made copies of those museum pieces considered too fragile to travel or to display, or those required for didactic and interpretation purposes. Building Three was a converted warehouse, the furthest away and the smallest of the museum's facilities, some blocks south of the main building.

The chief of Reproductions, Frantisek Kaliman—or Caliban as he was universally known by the staff—was the genius behind the department's success. He was from the old Czechoslovakia. Nobody knew his age; he had escaped the ideological pincers of the '68 and had come to the museum after a brief western-orientation in Vienna. He was short, bent, withered, and incredibly deteriorated.

After more than 40 years in the English-speaking world, Caliban's knowledge of the language was yet rudimentary. He did his shopping by pointing, he spoke only Czech among his cronies. A tax service did his returns. He wasted no time with any verb tense but the infinitive, although an occasional first-person singular might creep in. His nouns numbered probably 150 and he had no knowledge of sentential connectives. His favourite word (although nobody had ever had the heart to tell him it wasn't English) was usèd, pronounced rather like yew-zed. It was a sort of universal verb substitute. But, like his namesake, Caliban could swear in English with great variety and virulent virtuosity. It was his strong suit.

For all his apparent inarticulateness, Caliban always managed to make his wishes known very clearly.

'Ahh, somebahdy usèd putting bolyester catalyst jee zers crize!' could be quite well understood by all his staff.

An everlasting half-burnt cigarette hung from the corner of Caliban's bristly mouth. His fingers were stained a lurid yellow. When people complained that he was smoking in a restricted area, it could quite justifiably be argued that nothing that damp and saliva-ridden could possibly be induced to burn. When he coughed, which happened about every 10 inhalations, it came from some fluid chamber deep in the centre of his very being. Decades of exposure to polyester and epoxy fumes appeared to have replaced living bronchial tissue with a fragile plastic composite. He coughed with a desperate tearing sound like the rending of soiled bed linen, and his breathing reminded awestruck listeners of a rural steam ploughing match. He seemed on the very edge of eternity and had been so as long as anyone in the museum could remember. Caliban went on forever.

For all his eccentricity and bodily foulness, Caliban came of a culture that engendered and encouraged the arts of the hand and the eye. He was an absolute genius with rubber mouldings, synthetic resins, and pigments.

His genius was one of Bill Anker's heaviest crosses...

Reproductions of valuable artifacts that had crossed the old Czech's workbench were capable of fooling even the curators who were their custodians. He could make mere plastic look, feel and heft like wood, stone, bone, metal... anything. He directed his technicians and trainees with an unrelenting discipline, for he was a perfectionist, and they loved him, and feared him, and revered him for it. Aspiring technicians from around the world lined up to apprentice with him. And they got the results he expected. His work was astonishingly realistic.

The skilled and exacting business of creating *trompe l'oeil* reproductions is potentially damaging to the objects themselves. In order to get an accurate impression of a surface it is necessary to apply a substance that will harden and take a detailed copy of the surface with it. And this substance must be benign. A museum object can be ruined by a material that either won't come off, comes off with some of the surface being copied, or comes off cleanly but leaves a residue.

Before the advances of modern chemical technology, it was considered impossible to replicate the delicate objects that comprised the core of the museum's collections. With the development of silicone rubbers all that changed. The RTV rubbers—shorthand for room temperature vulcanizing—can be poured onto any surface as a liquid of any viscosity you desire and then, when cured or hardened, they can be peeled off revealing an extraordinary fineness of detail.

Copies are made from these rubber molds using pigmented epoxy or polyester resins, backed with fiberglass for strength. To give the copies the correct feel, or heft, they are sometimes made hollow and backfilled with denser materials balanced to give the correct density. Final touches include the addition of further thin coats of pigment, thick enough to provide colour, but not so thick as to obscure fine detail.

The large staff compliment and the state-of-the-art technical equipment of the Reproductions Department were a direct result of the condition of the main museum building.

And the power of the Conservation Department.

In the Museum of Personkind, conservation staff had real power; they were above the rest, they knew it, and they were not all that reticent in telling people. Many's the curator who had been more than pissed off by being told how to handle an object correctly, for example. Or being told more about its constituents and technology than she knew, or cared to know. And the conservators seemed to be everywhere, and to have their fingers (white gloved) in everybody else's business. They wagged fingers at clumsy researchers, they admonished display technicians, they lectured security guards and guides, they monitored everybody's environment. Their chief, Mr Easel, was, of course, the wielder of the reign of terror that held all museum departments accountable and subservient.

Museum conservation is an old discipline with a new twist. Ever since people have been collecting things they have also taken measures to preserve them. Restorers have been employed for centuries by rich patrons, such as merchants, kings, popes, and other well-heeled bullies of the same sort. But restoration caused irreversible change, so by preserving revered and treasured objects they were actually transforming them.

The 19th century saw a sea change in practice. Scientific techniques

26

began to be applied to problems of deterioration, while the stories that historic objects could tell became important. By the middle of the 20th century science was powerfully employed in the service of art. Museum conservation became the perfect combination of art and science, requiring an understanding and a control of both. Now it became the analytical and pragmatic blended with the manipulation of tools, materials and techniques. The old hand-oriented restorer gave way to the book-oriented conservator.

A wide-ranging technical literature grew out of museum research and study, with conservators and scientists alike contributing to such international journals of record as *Museum Conservation Studies* and *Recent Setbacks in Conservation*.

Museum conservation became an academic discipline.

A chief advance in conservation science was the understanding and control of the museum environment. In the Museum of Personkind's case, control of humidity was an ongoing and insuperable nightmare.

Some years ago, museum staff had noticed fresh cracks in a few wooden objects on display in the main building, and a meeting had been called seeking advice and direction. Around the large table in the fifth-floor boardroom sat a conservator, the managers of Infrastructure Support and Corporate and Financial Services, and a heating and ventilating engineer from Axlerod, Ratchet and Paul Inc. The two managers were suited, grey, unidimensional, and clearly not enjoying being there.

The conservator outlined the issue for the benefit of the managers: 'When the relative humidity of the air changes, organic materials, like wood, skin, and paper, react. Wood's the worst; as the humidity rises, the cellulose of the wood takes on water, and the object swells. When the humidity falls, it's the opposite; you get shrinkage. And this happens day and night because when the temperature falls, humidity rises.'

'Exactly,' said the consultant engineer. 'That's why old haunted houses creak at night. It ain't ghosts. It's all that wood trying to get comfortable!' He grinned into the vacuum.

'Yes, and sudden changes are even worse than day and night variations,' the conservator agreed. 'A quickly moving rainstorm will catapult the relative humidity up to 100% in minutes.'

'And, of course, there's low humidity in the winter,' observed the manager of Financial Services dryly.

'Sure. The annual variations are the long-term problem. In the winter the relative humidity difference between the outside air at, say, minus 20°C and the inside air at plus 20°C will be massive. Take a volume of that outside air and heat it up to room temperature and you get relative humidities in single digits!'

'Your worst symptoms would be a crispy nose, dry skin and shocks from static electricity,' said the engineer. 'But wood feels comfortable at a relative humidity of 50%, so those conditions are hell.'

'Wood splits and warps, delicate painted surfaces crack and flake away, you name it,' was the conservator's cheery opinion. Conservators of the old school love this; it means more things to have on the bench and fix.

'Yes, but we monitor the environment, don't we?' asked Infrastructure Support. 'Wherever you go in the museum there are these thingies for measuring RH.'

'Of course we *monitor* it,' replied the conservator. 'But that doesn't mean we're *doing* anything about it. Doesn't mean we're controlling it.' (And in an aside to himself: Just like personnel issues; monitor us all with morale surveys, worker satisfaction levels and bullshit, and then do screw all about any of it.)

'Well, you can't *do* anything, really,' put in the engineer. 'Old buildings just weren't designed for humidity control. It's really only in the last couple of decades that this problem came up. Buildings were always designed for people comfort.'

'You mean, keeping the building at the right temperature?' asked Financial Services.

'Exactly. Keep the occupants comfortable and let the relative humidity go where it wants. Museum artifact comfort just didn't come into it. See, if you try to humidify an old building like this the water vapour just pours out. In winter it freezes within the walls, causing frost spalling; bits falling off when the ice expands as it freezes. Then, of course, water condensing in the walls causes all kinds of mould growth, some of it toxic.'

'Can't you insert vapour barriers?'

'Well, you can retrofit old buildings with vapour barriers, but it's always expensive, and most often impossible.'

'What d'you mean, impossible?' asked the manager of Financial Services, wondering where the hell this discussion was going. 'What steps would need to be taken to control the RH in the main building?

That's what we called this meeting for!'

'Well, not impossible exactly,' backtracked the engineer a little. 'It would mean finding some way of insulating the old limestone walls, then all the windows—historic features of a designated heritage building, I don't need to remind you—would have to go, the roof would need to be torn off and replaced, and you'd need highly impermeable vapour barriers, otherwise all that humidity has to go somewhere. Like I said, dangerous levels of mould growth in the spring, and people on the sidewalk getting dinged by bits of building in winter. You're looking at 50 million at least. A new building might even be cheaper.'

'Yeah, that's true,' replied the conservator. 'When we did Building Four, the initial budget got blown out of the water. Remember, we had the initial estimate of...'

'All right, all right!' interrupted Financial Services, thoroughly rattled. 'We're not here to discuss other building projects.'

Upgrading Building Four had proved to be a complete fiasco, due mostly to the naivety of the originators of the project—ill-informed and gung-ho museum staff who thought that tearing a building to bits and putting it back together, while staff were still working in it, didn't need much thought—and the blistering incompetence of the Public Works Department who fumbled the ball repeatedly. The budget had, indeed, gone orbital and the timeline had extended over half a decade, while tongues were blackened and pants worn out at the knees on the carpets of the State Ministry of Finance. The museum could only thank God that no forensic audit had been performed. Heads would have become detached...

'So, where do we go from here?' continued the manager of Financial Services, knowing by now exactly what the answer was going to be.

'Maybe, be more selective in what we display in the galleries?' suggested the conservator. And there, at that time, the matter had been laid to rest. Characteristically, a decision was made to make no decision.

The man who had so callously sacked the Carpenter thoroughly enjoyed his power as chief of Conservation. And he had no hesitation in using the humidity control mess of the main building to his advantage.

Easel was one of those careless speakers for whom elision must have been coined. He used any expedient available to get to the end of a word as quickly as possible, slicing vowels and consonants with

29

abandon. He had the greatest difficulty with the letter T, so for work on his teeth he visited the dennis, he used barrys in his flashlight, and he referred to terrorists as terrace. He also enjoyed blowing wildlife to pieces, a practice he referred to as hunning.

Easel exerted enormous control over people, so when decisions on the wellbeing of the collections—or indeed any other aspect of the museum's running—were being made, it was much easier for all concerned to go with the flow, and not challenge him. He was aided by a particularly pliable director who had secrets to hide, and a management committee that liked peace and quiet. So, over the years, Easel's sphere of influence and control had extended far beyond the Conservation Department. It was this web of control that the conservation staff enjoyed, including computer databases, the registration department, display design and security, artifact handling, and many other aspects of routine museum operation.

His staff worked smoothly and cooperated willingly with Easel. He was one of those people who knew which button to push, so he could engender elation or misery in the recipient of his attention just as he chose. He could play people. And, provided his staff were fully on his side, he left them to concentrate on looking after the museum objects and their many other extraneous duties. He charmed them to toe his line and do exactly as he wished. If they bowed their will to his—and he made it seem like such good sense—the light would shine from their every aperture. He would protect them, and his own views reflected in them, from anybody and anything. Those who aligned themselves with him became a closed, exclusive and repressed group, always treated with metaphorical white gloves by the rest of the museum staff.

Behind his back, the other staff called Easel the Jim Jones of Conservation, and wondered how long it would be before he started mixing a batch of grape Kool-Aid.

But good luck to those individuals who had some independence of thought or judgement, and had the temerity to express their views. He turned on these people like a rabid skunk, and from that point onward they could do no right. He shunned them in public, he spread malicious rumours about them, and eventually reduced them to the point where they resigned in tears, disgust or relief. Unlike conservation treatments, his decisions were irreversible; once on his list you were finished. The Carpenter had discovered this to his cost.

Easel exuded an almost palpable fog of hatred. He had no conscience. He craved power over people. He enjoyed making them miserable. There is much analysis of such damaged people these days: was it his early home life, or perhaps a chemical imbalance? Was there some trauma in his young years; did his mummy drink, did his daddy beat him up?

The staff's opinion was simpler and unanimous; the man was an asshole.

Good conservation required stable relative humidity for the displays in the main building, while the heating and ventilating engineers demonstrated the impossibility of maintaining such conditions. This impasse might have remained indefinitely, had not Easel's lust for power come into play.

Over a period of years, under Easel's pernicious control, all 98 of those delicate and susceptible pieces of the Treaty Bluff collection became slowly replaced with plastic hymns to reproductive genius. Fragile 'wooden' bowls of pigmented polyester resin fooled the senses; masks were skin-deep real, with fiberglass below; every delicately carved item became a simulacrum, deceiving the eye and the mind. So wild were the humidity fluctuations that W.W. Easel had deemed almost every artifact to be in imminent danger of decease. None remained in their display cases.

To Easel's credit, it was he who had discovered Frantisek Kaliman labouring away making plastic reproductions for a local museum's Pre-School Museum Awareness Program. It is far better to give the children plastic artifacts to belabour each other with, than real ones. Even so, a parent had filed a suit on the grounds that a real stone peace pipe would have shattered on her child's head, rather than remaining intact and leaving a sizable dent. The case never went to court, but Caliban was glad to make a move elsewhere.

The conservators working under Easel were utterly in the thrall of their charismatic leader, and they became anal retentive to a degree. They took more than seriously the injunctions of their profession, preserving artifacts from all possible harm by systematically sequestering them in ideal conditions. Ideal for the artifacts, that is. The objects taken from the displays were stored in acid-free containers in their darkened warehouse in Building Four, with accurate control over all environmental factors. Access to their dedicated storage area was restricted to a very few carefully vetted staff members.

Photographs, written documentation, and drawings of the objects could be used by curators, historians, and students alike. Easel insisted on it. There was never any need to touch the real artifacts. They could, indeed, be preserved for eternity. Or even longer. Easel and his devotees presided over their hoard like white-gloved priests, with sterile lab coats buttoned, and with soulful El Greco eyes raised to heaven.

Nobody outside a small cadre of museum staff knew the extent of this systematic substitution. Only the reproductions staff, the staff of conservation, and the director and his chief curator knew what had been going on. The other curators didn't suspect, and anyway it wasn't their field. It was someone else's problem. No other member of staff in the entire museum knew. And, the Board of Trustees, on its regular visits to the neo-Classical pile for a glass of wine and little sausages on sticks, especially had no inkling of the fact that the awesome works of Person on display were a hollow sham. The 75th anniversary celebration had been a comprehensive fraud.

Gradually, as it grew upon those people in the know that the whole glorious display of human artistic genius that the Treaty Bluff collection represented had become largely plastic and quite modern, a fear and embarrassment factor had set in. In addition to their terror of Easel and what he might do to them, how could any of them admit that for the last decade the museum visitor had been thoroughly swindled? How to explain to the Board of Trustees that the artifacts that had caused them to pause, skewered sausage in hand, were in fact located in a disused wiener plant in lower town... without losing your job?

Over the years, since he had learned of it by accident, this horrible secret had made Bill Anker want to get on the wire to Solomon as possibly the only mortal in history qualified to deal with it. Why did he have to be faced with this nasty moral and ethical dilemma? Why was he the inheritor of such a policy, if policy it could be called? It was a policy that would lead to agonies unimaginable, and consequences dire.

It was the museum's best kept secret.

And yet another of Bill Anker's heavy crosses.

CHAPTER FIVE

I'm the only one who does any real work around here! thought Stephanie Chang. No, that was a bit unfair. But she was the only conservator who still did treatments on museum artifacts. That she did know. It was strange when you thought about it. The whole object of conservation when she had started her training, not all that long ago, was to bring objects back into good stable condition and to keep them that way. It was restoration, in that you got out your tools and brushes, your solvents and your glues, and you worked on the object. Except, unlike old fashioned restoration, you did the work with a systematic documentary approach, and you understood the chemical and physical characteristics of the materials. That, to her way of thinking, was the new science of conservation. Of course, you had to know why the object was in this condition, and what had happened to it, so it wouldn't return to that state in the future.

But it did seem to her that her colleagues had taken the preventive aspect of the business so far that they never actually did anything to an object. They monitored, they measured, they checked, they tested, and they performed a multitude of tasks around the collections, but they never actually rolled up the sleeves and plunged in. The amount of time they all spent on their brand-new computers was inordinate. She relished the French pun.

Being a stickler for accurate documentation, the often-misused term 'preventative' conservation irritated her. 'Preventative' was a noun, so preventative conservation had to be the action of conserving preventatives. While she was not aware of any specialization in the field of rubber appliance treatment, she didn't dismiss the existence of such a refined career.

Stephanie was a senior conservator reporting directly to Mr Easel. When she stepped back a bit from her busy daily life, she realized how fortunate she was. She was a little over 30 with a great job, doing what she loved, and with a nice place in the centre of town. She also had a new guy who really meant something to her, and a strongly supportive boss. *So, lighten up on the frustration and count your blessings!* It was annoying, though.

She had a huge list of treatments that needed doing; most of them cleaning and minor repair, but before that she had a complex procedure to perform on a fragile wooden object. It was a hardwood rattle, so badly eaten by insects that it was a hollow shell.

She would use vacuum impregnation, soaking the object in a synthetic resin and solvent solution while drawing out the air. She and an intern were preparing the chemicals and equipment as these thoughts crossed her mind.

'Just pass me the end of that hose, will you?' she asked the intern. 'That's it. Now, it's connected to the vacuum pump, so a little grease on these seals and we'll be almost ready.'

For objects in this condition, soaking in a resin solution is essential, but it takes a good deal of courage. Stephanie was only too aware that she was about to alter permanently a museum object, and do something to it that was potentially dangerous to its future wellbeing. There would be no going back.

Not all staff, she felt, had the confidence for this kind of work. Though she would never, ever, express this to any of them, she felt that it was a lack of courage. Handwork had never been important to them in their academic careers, and because it was something that couldn't easily be graded and measured, the colleges tended to dismiss it. None of the other conservation staff at the Museum of Personkind had worked consistently with their hands, and they were uncomfortable when called upon to do so.

That's why they plunged into the multitude of tasks that Mr Easel's all-encompassing regime had invented over the years. And, you know, sometimes she felt that they looked down on her because she wasn't afraid to get her hands dirty. Ah, well. Things could be a lot worse. She tightened a hose clip.

The boss, though, was a sensitive issue. She knew there was friction and bad feelings, of course—and, yes, Mr Easel could be a complete bastard—but because she worked for him, and because she liked her job, she toed his line. If you were on his team he would support you to the ends of the Earth. And she was most definitely on his team because the alternative wasn't to be thought about. She knew that Mr Easel didn't agree with her, or any of the others, associating too closely with the rest of the staff, and she also knew that champion though he was, he could switch sides irreversibly if he was crossed. A bit of a tightrope, but so far, no slips.

She thought briefly of the Carpenter as she continued mechanically to set up the apparatus. Mr Easel had set her straight on him! She had had no idea! He had seemed like such a nice guy and a great craftsman; she had definitely got on okay with him, and things might easily have developed. Just shows what false impressions some people can make.

The image of that young man in her mind turned her thoughts to Brian, her latest. She would be seeing him again this afternoon. Like most of the lower-level staff, she worked only until noon on Mondays and made up for it on Saturday morning. Monday afternoons were a good time to get in the groceries, make appointments; all the things that were easy on Monday, difficult on Saturday. In her department, only Mr Easel worked all day Monday, but then she saw him on Saturdays as well. These extra hours, mostly at the computer monitor, were clearly a sign of his devotion to the museum and to his staff.

She and Brian had been seeing a lot of each other since they first met, and it looked like continuing for a good long time, touch wood. It was funny how they had met. People phoned up the museum from time to time to ask questions about their antiques—their market value, how to care for them, and so on—but not many phoned with technical questions on restoration. Brian Connolly was restoring an old car, a 1936 Hudson, and he wanted to know about the preservation and repair of old woodwork. As she was the lab's wood specialist, the call had been directed to her. One thing (as they say) led to another. I bet he never thought while preserving his rotten old Hudson he would end up with my naked legs wrapped around his waist, heels digging into the small of his back...

'Hey, Steff! You're miles away!' The intern she was supposed to be instructing was holding a vacuum hose expectantly.

'Sorry, I was just thinking of an interesting impregnation procedure. Where were we?'

They completed setting up the apparatus, and began the delicate task of vacuum impregnation.

A battery of tests had already been performed on the rattle to ensure that the chosen solvent and synthetic resin combination was compatible and would do no harm, and a great deal of literature research had also been done to review previous treatments and to ensure the long-term viability of the result.

Stephanie's research had raised an interesting and potentially contentious issue. According to the treatment documentation in the museum Registry, it appeared that Mr Easel had done such an impregnation years ago on a mask of the Hare, the cult figure known as N'ufnīvah, but he had used cellulose nitrate, a material both harmful and quite dangerous, mainly because it was highly flammable.

She was also shocked at the poor quality of his documentation. For one who was so critical of the documentation of other staff, talk about the pot and the kettle...

But of immediate concern, would he notice that she had used a different material during his cursory review of her work? And would he ask her to justify her choice? This was one of those situations where you just pulled your head in and hoped for the best.

It was now time to immerse the rattle, hung with weights on nylon lines, in a large glass container full of the resin solution. Stephanie placed a lid on the container, which sealed it tightly, and turned on the vacuum pump connected to the chamber by the hose. As the air above the solution was removed, they could see the air inside all the insect tunnels bubbling and frothing its way to the surface. Then, when the vacuum was briefly but gently released, the solvent would rush in to take the place of the evacuated air. Several such cycles were necessary before no more bubbles could be coaxed from the wood. Once this was assured, Stephanie removed the rattle from the container, and with the intern's help moved it onto a grating suspended above a tray of solution.

She then left the object to drain in the fume hood until no more solution came out. It was then weighed on a digital scale and set aside under a polyethylene cover for drying and monitoring. Over several weeks the solvent would evaporate, leaving the resin within the wood. The rattle would be weighed every day so that the evaporation could be plotted on a graph. Once the line was flat, drying was considered done. Now the object would weigh as much, perhaps more, than when the wood was fresh, but in this iteration it was essentially made of plastic. An irreversible change, but done because the alternative would be to lose the rattle entirely through inevitable decay.

'That's it for the day,' smiled Stephanie as she tidied up the equipment and washed her hands. 'It's just before noon. Time for a quick lunch, then out for the afternoon. See you tomorrow!'

Stephanie and Brian met outside the main doors of the Town Centre at 1:00 p.m. The annual Antique Auto Show was on all this week and she had agreed to indulge his interest. In truth, she was not as overwhelmed by old cars as she had led him to believe when they first met, but that was something that could be dealt with later. There were more important things about him to be interested in, and rotten wood and greasy bits of engine were not among them. So, she would simulate an interest, but not feel too bad about it because of the joy she felt in his company.

Unfortunately, the car show would precipitate the first of a string of petty disagreements as their relationship progressed. It was silly really.

They elbowed their way through the throngs of spectators surrounding the gleaming examples of wheeled chrome and enamel. Brian knew one of the exhibitors here, and so Stephanie was introduced to the nitty-gritty of his hobby and passion. As she contemplated an immaculately restored automobile from the 1930s, she couldn't help comparing the owner's approach with her own. For this guy, the original object was the starting point for creativity; it was almost a bare canvas upon which he could practice his art: new paintwork, new upholstery, modern electrics, hydraulic brakes, the list went on.

In her work she intervened only reluctantly, respecting the original materials and state of the object, and eschewing creativity wherever it reared its unscientific head. Her additions—those that her code of ethics and individual sensibility allowed her to introduce—were easily distinguishable and, wherever possible, removable. His were permanent additions to the concept of the builder, and in many cases improvements on the original design. She didn't like it very much.

Brian asked her what she thought of the restoration, and she was just a bit too candid.

'Well, I think it's wrong. It doesn't matter what the artifact is, it should show its age and all the things it's been through. Otherwise, you're wiping out all that history and trying to find some totally imaginary previous state.'

'What do you mean 'imaginary?' Jeez, you've been at that bloody museum too long.'

'At least that bloody museum has taught me to think!' she snapped back, as auto aficionados around them dragged their eyes away from the cars.

'Hey, hey, hey,' he soothed, placing his hands on her shoulders. 'Let's save our first disagreement for something important. Maybe I shouldn't have said that about the museum, but it's a pretty tight-assed place, y'know. You may not believe it, but the past isn't something you can pin down on a piece of cork and keep forever.'

'But... well, my view—the museum view—is valid too,' she argued.

'I never said it wasn't. But you can't assume it's better—more moral or ethical or something—it's just different, that's all.'

'I never mentioned ethics!'

'Okay. Don't get on a high horse about it. And don't forget, when they pin butterflies on a piece of cork, they poison them first.'

'What's that supposed to mean?'

'I'm just saying that your museum environment is not all it's cracked up to be. It's dead and it's out of touch with the real world.'

'Well, I don't live in there! I do go home nights, you know!'

They walked through the crowd in silence, not really paying much attention to the gleaming exhibits, each absorbed in their own thoughts.

Monday afternoon was turning out rather shitty after all.

CHAPTER SIX

I t was a longstanding tradition, and an unchallenged assumption, that the director of the Museum of Personkind would be a museum professional, and not a government bureaucrat. This was very unusual, because in most such hierarchies, vacancies are filled laterally, from a limited pool of smooth operators scratching each other's backs in circles. So, whether the incumbent knows anything about the job or the functions of the employees below him is simply not as issue. And most observers at the lower and middle working levels agree that during their terms of office these glib figureheads rarely deign to learn much about what goes on below them anyway.

The structure of Bill Anker's organization dated from a previous era when it seemed natural that the boss should be a professional in the field. It would probably not be long before this old fashioned—and therefore deeply suspicious—state of affairs was rectified. The new wave was, in fact, working upwards. Immediately below Anker's level was the management committee; five glorified office boys striking a paper wedge between him and the professionals two levels below. They managed the five divisions of the museum: Human Resources, Professional Activities, Corporate and Financial Services, Infrastructure Support, and Public Programs. These were the sort of people who rise in the sort of place the museum was. None had extensive professional experience, and certainly not in the areas they now managed. Nor was it necessary. Each had aspired to the management level by having that curious gift of appearing to be highly organized in a paper and computer fashion, while not actually doing anything much. Theirs was the art of writing reports that will never be read, producing spreadsheets that will never be analyzed, and of deferring decisions until somebody else makes them, or until the problem goes away. They were all middle-aged white men, of course; the museum was a testocracy. The staff called them the Gray Mafia. These nonentities hardly feature in this story.

As with most other 'progressive' organizations, re-org smoothies had blown through in the latter years of the 20th century, resulting in massive disruption, dubious results, and big bucks for the perpetrators, who had no more qualifications than the ability to drive a nail into a wall above a shingle that said 'business consultant.'

These consultants were the sort of people who said pruh-cess-eez instead of processes. (Doubtless, if they took more than one recess, they would be re-cess-eez.) Paradigm was the word on everybody's lips. Dynamic staff focus groups using decision-making protocols retooled the entire organization from reporting structure to cafeteria doughnuts. Different batches of staff, rotated in and out of committees, would sit around for hours staring at a whiteboard covered with little yellow sticky things, while votes were tabulated and fatuous suggestions given the full weight of mature thought and mathematical weighting. Orders for fat felt-tip pens and flip charts and the new-fangled Post-it notes soared. The new name of the museum was one of the early triumphs of the focus group approach to problem solving. It is significant that not one member of the business consultants or the museum's administrators could boast even a Bachelor's degree in business administration, let alone an MBA, which is the starting qualification for running a chip wagon.

Since this reorganization, a wide variety of made-up occupations came into being, created by people who enjoyed organizing other people. The number of extraneous committees in an institution can be a very reliable guide to the competence of its management. (Another reliable indicator is a comparison of the budget for marketing with the one for preservation of collections; if marketing gets more per capita, you know where the museum stands.)

The Museum of Personkind had dozens of extraneous committees. The Workplace Health and Safety Committee, with its 12 members who met every week, was typical. The WHISC (how they loved acronyms!) decided one day to focus on the safety of office and lab chairs. Specifically, the number of wheels. Yes, ever since the invention of the wheel the ideal number of them to put on a vehicle has been four. Like, one at each corner? But that simply wasn't good enough anymore. No siree! According to 'code' office chairs were obliged to have five wheels, to 'make them safer.' Nobody had done a survey to determine whether there were figures that indicated an alarming trend in workplace injuries incurred by office and lab workers falling off their chairs. Or even a blip. Nor had they done the math or the physics.

A small group of disgruntled employees, who liked their old chairs and didn't want to part with them, had done a study of the new chair safety code. After much wheedling, their chairperson (an annoying smart aleck who had a gift for telling people things he thought they really ought to know in as satirical a fashion as possible) was permitted to present the group's findings at one of the Gray Mafia's weekly meetings.

He told them that with a four-wheeled chair, there are four potential positions where tipping might be a hazard—at 90, 180, 270 and 360 degrees respectively—whereas with five wheels, the number of hazardous positions is increased to five—72, 144, 216, 288, and 360 degrees respectively. Clearly, the more wheels, the greater the hazard.

The Chair (five wheels) of the Management Committee thanked him for taking the time and trouble to point out these vital concerns to them, and once the door closed behind him, resumed the meeting as if nothing had happened. The last thing they wanted was some smartass staff group showing them that their Workplace Health and Safety Committee might be wrong.

So, the result of the group's presentation to the management committee was the rapid processing by the subcommittee responsible for interpreting 'code' of a large order for five-wheeled chairs. This incurred a great deal of unnecessary expense for the museum, and poured large amounts of cash into the coffers of chair manu-facturers, who were laughing all the way to the bank. Surplus stores throughout the town had great deals on obsolete but scarcely used chairs. Many hardy souls in the general public, not frightened away by four-wheeled chair accident horror stories, snapped up the bargains.

The half dozen head curators reported to the manager of professional services. They specialized in the fields of ethnology, anthropology, archaeology, history, and folk culture. Each of these heads held court over a gaggle of assistant curators, researchers, collections managers, registrars and interns. Among other recommendations, the amoebic and pervasive focus groups had decided that communication between the various curatorial sections and the management committee would be affected and expedited by means of a delegated temporary chief curator. This lucky soul would report to the Gray Mafia on behalf of the head curators.

At the end of a year a fresh head curator would be rotated into the position. It paid no more, and the extra duties effectively precluded the pursuit of one's profession for the duration. As with all Byzantine bureaucracies it was cumbersome, time consuming and open to abuse. In the hands of the managers and Bill Anker their director it was also screamingly frustrating.

For the first two years of its existence, the rotating chief curator position was tolerated. However, on the third year it came the turn of Rourke Mutcer, the new curator of history, to occupy the position. Unlike his colleagues, who loathed being removed from their professional duties in order to attend interminable meetings and read nonsensical and issueless reports ripe for the shredder, Mutcer was ready and eager to grasp advancement and hang onto it. In this role he could be almost a manager among managers. Moreover, he had no intention of being rotated out of the position in 12 months. In this he was abetted by two factors: his five curatorial colleagues who would gladly forego the honour, and that information he possessed concerning a certain disreputable action of the director.

The information involved an incident with fire, and the secret of those 98 reproductions in the Treaty Bluff collection, and the way in which he and his director had come to know about them. He used this shared knowledge only sparingly, but the evidence of it was stored away in his filing cabinet, ready for use whenever necessary. Unknown to his director, he also had some scurrilous personal information on file as well. You never know when you might need it!

At the close of his term Mutcer had merely suggested to his colleagues that, if they wished, he would continue in service to them in this undesirable, but clearly necessary, duty. They had agreed, not because they wished him well, but because they wanted simply to be left alone. Easel, the chief of conservation, also saw advantage in backing him because he was potentially just as pliable as Anker. Easel didn't give a damn who was at the top of the heap as long as whoever it was did as he was told. Anker himself had been persuaded of the eminent sensibility of keeping Mutcer as chief curator with scarcely any need for the application of pressure.

Rourke Mutcer could be thoroughly charming and he used this attribute well. But his charm and persuasiveness were always precarious because they could so easily be destroyed by close proximity. No matter what he did in the way of personal hygiene, he always smelt like a slightly gamy joint of pork. He had suffered this affliction for years and no dermatologist, dietician, allergist or homeopath had been able to make any impression on it. No amount of deodorant could overcome it. Nor could special soaps. And he had tried!

The miasma that surrounded him was in such contrast to his charm that it struck one with the same sense of tragedy as a suddenly paralyzed athlete... or an altruistic politician. Until one knew him better, of course. Behind his back he was given the nickname Pork.

Perhaps his aura was the reason why he chose blackmail and manipulation; they weren't so subject to rank interference. Mutcer had one little weakness. He carried a hip flask of strong spirits with him wherever he went, and he nipped on it frequently. He was under the mistaken impression that nobody knew. People always know.

A few staff, perceptive of Mutcer's potential future in the institution, toadied to him disgracefully. These he used and discarded, and it was more then they deserved. Most loathed but tolerated him. Caliban found him offensive and was never tired of saying so. His opinion of Mutcer was:

'Is asshole looking place shit. Him no usèd shit on me never never never jee zers crize.'

Caliban also knew the secret of fire and, of course, was closely acquainted with those reproductions...

Chapter Seven

R ourke Mutcer lusted after Bill Anker's job, and he lusted after a new museum in which to strut and preen. But his passion was unrequited. He was at an impasse, frustrated and unsure of his next move. It had been ideal to watch Anker build the pressure for a new museum building, to sit on his committee for years and watch all the spadework being done, knowing that he could wait in the wings and choose his moment to topple the bald little prick when the time came.

But now one shoddy memo had dashed his hope of a new museum, and the whole idea of ousting Anker and taking his place had lost its allure. Did he really want to be director of this shabby, second-rate collection of substandard shanties? No. New director and new museum went hand-in-hand.

Meanwhile, Mutcer's lust for this delicious double culmination of his career was not lost on Woodrow Wilson Easel. Easel lusted for control over people, not institutions and organizations. He craved the raw ecstasy that comes from making people do what you want, especially against their will or better nature. Psychological rape was his style. Sure, if Mutcer wanted a shove to get where he wanted to go, why not give it to him, as long as he was indebted forever to his benefactor? Besides, helping him would also bring Easel's own agenda along very nicely.

He'd had his staff rig the building report to make it look as if everything was okay because he liked things just the way they were. He felt his web of power could easily be disrupted by new buildings, new org structures, changes in routines; anything new and different was potentially dangerous. But now he was changing his mind. A new building might be okay if the conditions were right...

Here was what needed dealing with: the secret and systematic substitution of the Treaty Bluff collection—so satisfying while it was being done—was potentially very dangerous to him. If it was discovered that the ones on display were fakes he might have a lot of answering to do. And when they were removed for display in a new museum, the cat would be out of the bag for sure. So far there was only a bunch of people in the know, and they were either too scared of the administration and the public, or too scared of Dubya Dubya Easel—the finest man who ever shit between shoe leather—to spill the beans. But if it became generally known, the crap would fly.

So here was a potential solution: if, just for example, the copies on display got accidentally destroyed—maybe a terrible and tragic fire—those in the know would keep their mouths shut and everybody else would believe the originals had gone up in smoke. And having the originals in his care, safe and sound, was a huge bargaining counter for the future. Once he revealed his skill and care in preserving them, building a new museum for them would be essential, and his role would be heroic!

So, if Mutcer wants to get ahead, maybe he should be persuaded of the advantages of staging a little accident and laying the blame somewhere else. New museum, new director, perfect! And Mutcer was the ideal tool; pliable as putty, desperate for a friend, aching for advancement, clever and subtle, and open for blackmail once he's well immersed. Better have a little talk with him.

In Easel's worldview it didn't matter how far you went; the end always justified the means. This groaning world's full of them.

While a display case was being tampered with upstairs, and one of his security guards was playing games, chief of Museum Security Lucien Limace sat at a greasy desk in his basement office oblivious. He reamed out his nose industriously. He didn't have much else to do and it kept his hands busy. He lived in an illness of fat, which he blamed on his glands, instead of the pizza and beer and hamburgers and fried chicken and more beer with which he fed his suety carcass.

The security of the museum looked after itself. Guard duty rounds had all been established years ago, burglar alarm systems were serviced by a contract with a security firm, display security was Conservation's problem, his underlings did all the meaningless but necessary paperwork, and the pay cheques rolled in regularly. Provided nothing happened to require his attention, Limace could sit back on his haunches in his windowless basement office and slide greasily towards retirement.

He shifted his bulk in his sticky wooden chair, and as he extended his legs his boots rustled and crunched on the piles of discarded fast-food wrappings under his desk.

He hadn't always been so lazy. He was naturally gifted that way, of course, but the craft had taken him years to perfect. Before he learned the skills of delegation and manipulation, he had even done some work himself. Those were the early days; he probably wouldn't know what to do now if he was told. And he wouldn't care anyway.

Somebody else's problem.

The manager of human resources was at fault for the nurture of Limace's slack, slug-mindedness. Complaints had been made about Limace (and Easel, of course) on a monotonous basis for years, but like his other colleagues in the Gray Mafia, this manager could play the old ceramic owl with the best of them.

Here's how it worked: a member of staff would go to his office to make a complaint. He would listen to the complaint and know that the substance of it was justified. At the same time, he would know that if he as much as slightly indicated that he was sympathetic to the complainant he would demonstrate weakness. On the other hand, he could not show even the slightest support for the one against whom the complaint was lodged either, because that would indicate that he condoned a behaviour that he knew to be wrong, while he also knew that the complainant would know that he knew it to be wrong. The resultant impasse created a cognitive dissonance between what obviously needed to be done, and what equally obviously never *would* get done. A coward can only handle such dissonance in one way: the eyes glaze over and fix in the middle distance, the face becomes devoid of expression, and the whole body becomes rigid and still. The complainants soon find themselves talking to—and eventually running down to a stop in front of—a china mantel ornament.

So, Limace's brand of sloth was tolerated, and even condoned by inaction. He could continue to pull down the paycheques and not be overly concerned about actually earning them.

But this would be the last day of his torpor.

Limace's woes would begin with Sue Tort. She had visited the museum a few weeks after checking out the 75th anniversary celebrations. She was even more pissed off now, and had begun hatching a plan to stage a protest. It was her calling; she'd been a professional protester for near on 30 years. Professional in the purest sense of the term; it was a full-time job. What money she got came from 'well-wishers,' and most of them as suspect as hell. Name a Cause in the last three decades and she'd been wedded to it. She had begun her protesting career in university, when she should have been pursuing an education. Instead, she espoused Causes; lots of them. The chief, and almost only, things all her schooling had taught her were to react negatively and to complain. Over the years she had developed a reputation as an organizer and planner of popular demonstrations. She had built up an extensive network of sympathizers, helpers, money providers and spies. So, once again, she pulled the strings and started the process rolling.

Monday was target day.

The ragged mob came marching toward the museum in straggling file. About 100 individuals, wrapped against the cold late afternoon November wind, flushed with the excitement of protest, carrying banners that read 'Give Them Back,' 'Theives' and 'Rites For Natives.' This miserable bunch gathered in the forecourt of the museum, where once the rich had stepped from their limousines and whisked up the steps into the old department store. The mob began a thin, bitter chanting.

'Give them back! Give them back!' they yelled in competition with diesel buses, sharp wind, and public indifference.

The most strident voice in the mob belonged to Sue Tort, right there in the front row. It was a scene out of the 1970s. It was shabby and rather sad.

Two police cars were parked across the road from the museum, and vehicles bearing the logos of local media showed the press and television had been tipped off. One of the protesters—a big Celtic looking character with red hair—set up a microphone and amplifier at the top of the stairs before the museum doors, and the mean-mouthed woman came forward.

'Are we gonna let them get away with this?' the thin speakers whooped and squeaked. 'Are we gonna let these curator thieves keep our original people's sacred treasures and stuff? What gives them the moral right to steal a people's heritage? Lissen! In the last 10 years this museum has been approached scores of times to return stuff what's not rightly theirs. They stole the Treaty Bluff Collection! They orter give it back! Know what the response has been? I'll tell you what the response has been! Nothing! Zee-ro! Not a peep!'

A number of the more passionate sorts yelled encouragement. The speaker continued:

'It's up to us! The time has come to demand justice! We do not move from here until we get action! Action!'

'Action! Action!' chanted the crowd, warming a little to their mission.

Flashes lit the facade of the museum; cameras panned. The

police stirred in their patrol cars, granules of sugar adhering to their chins, crumbs dusting their uniforms.

'*Action! Action!*'

The front door security guard had only finished dealing with Easel and the loose screws an hour ago, and this was the last thing he wanted to disturb his quiet afternoon in the front booth. On hearing the row outside, he stepped out of his glass booth, peeped through the spy hole in the great oaken front door, and made a masterly misanalysis of the situation. The spy hole was small, and the glass distorted the view. The crowd was magnified to a mob. He phoned Lucien Limace, his boss, in the basement and blurted out:

'Thousands of 'em! Heading for the museum! There's TV an' papers an' dozens of cop cars!'

'Shut up an' tell me what the hell you're talkin' about, for Christ's sake!' growled Limace with scant attention to logic. Clear thought wasn't at the top of his agenda at the moment.

'Thousandsa demonstrators, cop cars, everything!'

'Thought I told you to shut up? Shit! Demonstrators, eh? Stay in your booth, lock the goddam' doors, an' wait there. I'll call the fuckin' director.'

The director's phone was busy. Shit! This meant moving. Panicked into action by events out of the ordinary, Limace set out for the director's office. The ancient elevator still wasn't working, so he began to negotiate the stairs. Delegation was so ingrained into his very flesh that even he was surprised to find himself jiggling up to the director's fifth-floor aerie. He lost his way twice, having not ventured up there for over five years. By the time he arrived at the mahogany-faced door with brass nameplate he was physically ill from the unaccustomed exercise, while lack of blood to his brain was causing hallucinations. He burst in and propped himself against the Dikk hat stand, pale, sweating and gasping for breath.

The 'fuckin' director' was still mourning his lost museum, and making useless phone calls to people he thought might be influential, but who had all gone home for the day anyway. (If he ever suspected how many times the copulatory adjective had been appended to his title he would have been mortified. But that's the price you pay for being a fuckin' director.)

Anker quickly angled his desk lamp upwards. All the signs of fear and panic in the security chief's heaving face communicated themselves to him, and because he had just that day received the bad news concerning his new museum plans, he was already in a delicate and vulnerable condition.

'Thousands er demonstrators... outside... yellin' fer blood... Cops... the whole bit. Whatcha gonna do about it...?' wheezed Limace as he collapsed sideways onto the broadloom in the ruins of the hat stand.

What Anker did was overreact in a characteristically ill-organized and inefficient fashion. With the help of the phone and the public address system he had the entire museum in a state of near panic within minutes. He fired off misleading and contradictory orders to whomever was in earshot, he had doors and windows bolted and barred. Emergency lighting was tested, fire alarms rang out, more police were called, and by some means that nobody could afterwards explain, three ambulances and the crews from four fire stations were dispatched to the scene.

Now synergism began to take effect. The ambulances and fire engines roaring through the streets, the TV cameras and press, all contributed to a sense of alarm. Crowds of office workers just released at going-home time poured towards the museum to swell the chanting demonstrators. Panic rumours of terrorist activity passed through the crowd. Traffic became snarled. Police, fire engines, and ambulances were unable to approach the scene of the disaster. They sat in the traffic with sirens wailing and hooting while their crews cursed and swore foully. In minutes the museum was surrounded by a roaring mob, a valiant few of whom still chanted *'Action! Action!'*

The spectators began to take up the chant. *'Action! Action!'* they bellowed, not one person in 10 knowing what the hell they were doing there or even what action was required.

From the fifth-floor window the vista was horrifying. All it lacked were the flaming torches of the peasants and a fugitive Baron Frankenstein. Anker looked down from his tower in horror. It was a nightmare scene fit to loosen the bowels of a bronze statue. He was stung into further irrational action.

He issued orders to Limace, now partially mobile but still on the floor of the office, to open the packing cases of the travelling exhibition *Arms Through the Ages*, which were stored in the loading bay. Limace rose to a wheezing vertical and tottered off. In a few minutes the entire security contingent was parading in the foyer, in front of Anker and most of the institution's staff, including Rourke Mutcer, armed with a most absurd array of display weaponry. Perspiring guards in shabby uniforms were loaded down with reproduction Brown Bess muskets, arquebuses, stone axes, and even Congreve rockets.

As they stood to receive their orders, the Museum Militia and their valiant general were startled by a thundering at the huge oak doors in the foyer.

'They'll never take us alive!' screamed Anker in a paroxysm of fear. 'The museum will go down with all buns glazing!'

The Museum Militia surged forward, facsimile plastic weapons clattering. The thunderous assault was repeated and Anker, elbowing aside his valiant force, opened the small security flap in the oaken door. A beefy-red, furious face appeared, horribly magnified and distorted.

'Open this bloody door and let us in, you clown!' rasped the chief of police who had forced his way to the door amidst a wedge of armoured riot police. 'And stop shining your head in my face!'

The chief of police had a long nose; well, cops did, didn't they? They were always poking them into places they weren't welcome. Mind you, he didn't do a hell of a lot of nosing around these days, having graduated to the desk some time back. He missed the old days a bit, but there are times when enough is enough. Even so, the museum intrigued him; you would think it'd be the last place for criminals to hang their shingles out, but you never knew.

Anker slid the bolts back and pulled the door open. The chief barged in followed by a phalanx of heavily armed cops, who swarmed into the foyer surrounding the security guards and chanting 'Hut, hut, hut.'

Riot shields clashed and billy clubs thumped. The guards laid down their display weapons sheepishly in front of eight sniggering policemen.

'Thank God you've come,' twittered Anker. 'We're under attack!'

The chief thrust his long, suspicious face down at Anker. 'I don't know what the hell's going on here and I don't think I want to know,' he said, 'but if you don't get out there and reason with that mob your ass won't be worth a nickel!'

'What do you mean, go out there?' wailed Anker. 'I'd get lynched. Anyway, the museum's closed today. It's Monday.'

'Now,' enunciated the chief, very slowly, 'if somebody does not go out and offer those demonstrators a modicum of negotiation, there will be *consequences*.' His patience was becoming... tested.

Anker thought quickly (something that panic aided and serenity suppressed). He couldn't do it! No, no, no! He hated public speaking, and besides the TV lights were angled all the wrong way. Better to send Mutcer. Yes, send Mutcer; he loved publicity, the oily bastard, and he could charm the panties off a nun. Especially out in the open air.

'Mutcer, you heard the chief. Do my... our... your duty.'

Normally Rourke Mutcer would have bridled at such an order and ignored it on principle. However, he saw the golden advantage of a good performance out there, while also showing up his director for a coward, so he agreed with a great show of reluctance. He did his *Burghers of Calais* impression; putting on the world-weary-martyr-turning-his-back-on-his-loved-ones-to-face-the-enemy expression, he plodded stoically to the great oak doors.

Outside the roar of the mob subsided as the doors swung fully back. Cameras flashed as Rourke Mutcer stood alone in front of the microphone, conscious of his role at a historic moment in the museum's history. He stood within a small semicircle of police reinforcements who were keeping the crowd back from the doors. Each one was armed and protected with a helmet, billy club and riot shield. He spread his hands in a papal benediction over the crowd. He drew breath to speak, deeply conscious of the moment.

'Friends,' he began. 'You have come before the museum today to protest a matter of great importance. We at the museum are attuned to your desires...'

The mutter of the crowd welled to a menacing rumble. He waited, timing his pause, until the sound subsided.

'But we cannot negotiate from this position.'

He was doing very well. He felt his control of the crowd strengthen. He drew breath slowly and with head thrown back, continued:

'But negotiate we can and must!'

Suddenly, at what must surely have been his moment of triumph, with the mob ductile before him, somebody launched a teargas grenade right at him. It bounced, smoking, off his shoulder and rolled into the crowd. A whole section of the mob to Mutcer's leeward staggered back, retching and gasping.

'Gas!' choked somebody in the crowd, and 'Chemical warfare!'

The police cordon broke. The panic-stricken mob scattered in all directions.

Mutcer flung himself on all fours as a hail of debris peppered the walls, and crawled for the door amid screaming pandemonium and running feet. Something caught him squarely on the side of the head, and he slid to the ground, his nether aperture emitting a squittering trumpet of alarm before the roar of the crowd faded...

Inside the building the Jonah at the centre of the disaster dithered and twittered. In unison the eight riot police raised their shields and forced a way out into the tempest. As an afterthought, just before the door closed on them, they slid the unconscious form of Mutcer back into the museum.

With chaos at its full height, a woman was seen approaching the museum, clearing a way through debris, shoving aside spectators and demonstrators like a Dreadnought taming the German Sea. She breasted the stairs, and once again the great oaken museum doors burst back. She stepped into the foyer, focused her gaze upon Anker and willed him to come forward to meet her.

With a voice that brooked no gainsay, she boomed to all present, 'We're leaving. This will all be dealt with in the morning.'

And taking the director's arm firmly in hers she hustled him from the scene. With Anker under tow, she ploughed through the seething riot again like a great icebreaker casting aside polar floes, and disappeared with him in the direction of the car park.

Doris Ironside-Anker of the naval Ironsides had made her appearance.

Sue Tort sat alone at a Melamine topped table in the dismal upstairs kitchen of a rundown dump on the east side of town. She stared at the sticky, vinyl tiled floor in dejection. As she identified herself with cause after cause, year after year, she became more bitter... and more resigned. Her mean mouth got meaner. The face got more lines.

She was getting too old for this game.

For all her energetic protests, she never saw any real change. Most people, when faced with a continual string of conspicuous failures, would just chuck it all in. Whales were still being harpooned, off-shore oil wells were still being drilled, tar sands still killing ducks, and the smelters were still spewing out crap. Clear-cut logging continued in the forests and industry still shat in the lakes. Climate summits were a joke. Why didn't she just chuck it all in?

Simple. Didn't know any other life.

But she never got results! Never! Yesterday's screw up was just about fuckin' typical. She shifted in her chair, swigged cold, stale coffee, and scratched herself coarsely under her small breasts. The ashtray was full.

Her co-organizer bounced into the kitchen. Terry O'Weight was her complete antithesis. Round faced, beaming, orange haired and huge, he was always overflowing with action, ever ready to topple ivory towers. On one of his well-rounded biceps was an elaborately tattooed cartouche, framing the word 'mother.' New acquaintances saw this as a reflection of warmth and filial affection from a loving youth. Until they looked at the other arm with its matching tattooed cartouche, framing the word 'fucker.' His grandfather was Irish-born and Terry had inherited all his excellence of wit, boisterousness and jovial good looks. Somebody else had inherited the brains.

'Holy shit, what a demo! What... a... demo! I never had so much fun since we wasted that computer lab! Ho lee shit!'

His mouth contained an almost permanent wad of chewing gum, which he replenished at regular intervals. He reeked of beer, cigarette smoke, and cheap peppermint.

'For Christ's sake shut up! You call that a success? Are we any nearer getting what we want? Are we, *shit!* We're much further away. Jus' when we had that stuffed up prick makin' promises! Think they'll negotiate now? And it's all your goddam' fault!'

She turned her face away in disgust.

'Me? Everythin' was fine until some asshole threw teargas. Holy jeez, did you ever see anything like it? Awe-some!'

'Oh, an' you didn't throw it eh?' she yelled. 'An' who's the stupid fuckhead who started shouting about chemical warfare? Who gets the whole fuckin' crowd in a panic just when we're getting some-where? You stupid shithead!'

'Bull... shit! They were choking and throwing up before I said any-thing. Anyway,' he continued meekly, 'lots of other people got teargas. Plenny left over from the last one remember.'

She subsided, glowering. Maybe he didn't start it, but she had her suspicions even so. He was a great lieutenant, but sometimes it was like wiping the chin of a toddler.

'I'm just bummed out with what the sponsors'll say, that's all.' This wasn't true. It was a good bet that the mess the protesters had made would have pleased them mightily.

'Who are the sponsors, anyway?'

'Dunno', she lied. 'An' you know I fuckin' don't know.' She lit another smoke.

It was a dumb question, and no matter how many times he asked it, the reply was always the same. Of course she knew, but there was a great deal of dissonance between her ideology and what she assumed was theirs. To keep peace in her own mind she was quite prepared to ignore the rationale for putting up the funding, but she knew it had nothing to do with rights or freedom from oppression. They paid; that was all that mattered. And, in the modern jargon they were results-oriented. Maybe a riot with bottles, stones, police, and teargas was right up their alley? She could only hope so.

O'Weight, on the other hand, found life impossible to take seriously. His role as Tort's lieutenant was ideal. For her, protest was a bitter trial, a sour and weary way of life that had become desperately addictive. For him it was a dream drug. As long as he was given action, excitement and shit-stirring he was happy. Between campaigns such as this one he could be in jerky and sullen withdrawal, and would drink even more than usual. But when action called, he would do exactly what he was told with a boisterous and laughing enthusiasm.

The world can thank God he was raised in ignorance of Irish history. Or anything else for that matter.

They made a perfect pair.

She never let him touch her. No matter how close they were, no matter what they went through together, he did not lay a finger on her.

She had a man once, years ago in university. Not like him. He had been a professional protester too, and she had admired him for it in the beginning. She had looked up to him, hung by him... but love? Who knows? It was fine, in its way, until it began to dawn on her that, for all his reaction to society, he was quite content to live off it like a louse. His one aim in nonconformance was the avoidance of lifting a finger. He did no work, as a form of protest; he didn't wash, as a form of protest; he stole, as a form of protest. Sometimes his protest caused him to spend days on end in bed.

Finally, she had snapped. She waited until he was in a drugged sleep one afternoon, piled all his stinking, unwashed clothes into the bathtub, doused them in barbecue starter, and dropped a match. She was out of the apartment and far away, never to return, by the time the evil, choking fumes had aroused the naked and furious layabout. It was a shame she couldn't have stayed to see his filthy, matted form shinning down a drainpipe into the crowded street below. A picture of his hairy bum, emerging from the third-floor window, surrounded by a halo of smoke, had appeared in the evening papers. Justice!

It had been a long, hard road of stupid, futile causes since then. Occasionally she wondered what Terry would be like, but she shoved the thought away.

She took a long drag on her cigarette. Her futility began to harden into resolve. The spore of an idea had begun to germinate on the agar of her mind. Her apotheosis would come when she could sit down at the bargaining table with these three-piece-and-tie jerks on equal terms. It would come! And she had the lever!

'Terry,' she said quietly, 'we're not done yet. They're gonna come begging to us, boy. They're gonna sit down and negotiate on our terms.'

'Oh, yeah? How?' He was puzzled.

'First off, we gotter find a way to get into that museum at night.'

O'Weight's expression passed slowly from cluelessness to sly know-all. He began grinning broadly.

'No problem!' he smirked while a smug look settled on his big, silly face. He obviously had some great secret that he couldn't wait to share.

'All right! Spill it! Don't have to keep me in fuckin' suspense.' She had no patience with him tonight. God, his total absence of guile was so childish sometimes.

'C'mon! What is it?'

'Well, some guy follered me from the demo to O'Donnell's in the market, and we got talking, see? Bought me a beer.'

She raised her eyebrows.

'*Some* beers... Basic'ly, he used to work at the museum, but he's real pissed off with them. Something they did to him, eh?'

Tort brightened up a little. Maybe the big oaf was onto something after all. 'So you think he might wanna help us? That what you're saying?'

'Dunno, but we can always give him a try. He give me his phone number,' he concluded smugly.

'Right! You're goin' to get in touch with him nice an' soon. Now, gimme another smoke and lissen to this...'

O'Weight was soon beaming and chuckling, ready for action. They hatched over the plot from as many angles as they could, and every time it sounded better! Even Tort began to smile.

Chapter Eight

I t was Tuesday around noon, and Rourke Mutcer was lolling in his office chair congratulating himself on being an extremely fortunate man in two ways. First, yesterday's riot. The entire staff of the museum had been behind stout oak doors when he had lost control of his audience. That was good. Then, when he regained consciousness, it was as a hero! People seemed to think only of his selflessness in stepping into the holocaust. Morons. His popularity wouldn't last long, but he would play it while it did. During the interrogation by the chief of police this morning, he made much of his saviour's role. In a sudden access of pseudo-charity, he even forbore blaming Anker for initiating the debacle, and for subsequently deserting the scene. Heroes don't stoop to such low tricks. Besides, he had grander plans for his soon-to-be ex-director.

And that's where his second piece of good fortune came in. Mr Easel had been to see him, and had suggested the most fantastic plan for furthering his directorial aims! And, as Easel had told him frankly, only a man of Mutcer's courage and steadfastness of purpose could pull it off. 'Rourke, my friend,' he had assured him, 'you, sir, are director material, and together we'll see to it!'

Mutcer's first-floor office was in the east wing of the main building, further along from the loading bay. Due to his bodily affliction, Mutcer had maneuvered for himself one of the few offices with opening windows. While most of the administration was on the fourth and fifth floors of the west wing, some overflow space had been occupied on this side. It was rather miserable in the winter. He looked out directly onto the car park at the rear of the museum. The rear loading bay door and the security booth were to the right, behind a dumpster which held waste from the cafeteria. When the weather was from the west—the prevailing wind—there was an atrocious competition of odours around his window. No winner had yet been declared.

The office of the chief curator bore few traces of his own academic career. The walls were covered with exhibition posters of shows that other museums had hosted. The features of Tutankhamun and Philip of Macedon stared down from adjacent walls. Pictures of ladies' fans, steam locomotives, antique musical instruments and the Book of

Kells promoted past curatorial triumphs for museums across the country and around the world. Near the door a ghastly array of coloured swatches advertised the detrimental effects of light on museum objects. Two filing cabinets, a thinly populated bookshelf, a computer table, and a desk occupied most of the floor space.

It was about time for the next phase of his plans to mature. So, our director wanted a new museum, did he? Well, he would get his new museum. But he wouldn't be director of it. No, sir! Thanks to W.W. Easel's generous help, Rourke Mutcer's name was on the door of that particular office! He knew that with Easel—the real power behind the wheels of the museum—supporting him, he couldn't fail. How good it felt to be so close to the true source! One of the boys! Fire! Yes, fire! Such an alluring metaphor for change!

But first it was necessary to lay some careful groundwork. He sat down in front of his computer and began typing. He was busy for nearly an hour creating several documents. He then got on the phone to Chief Limace in his cave in the basement.

'Loosh'n,' he said, holding the major document before him. 'That report on the fire hazards you wrote for the director three years ago was never signed.'

'Report? What report? I never wrote nothin' about any fire 'azards.'

This was true; there was no extant evidence that Limace had ever written anything.

'Really? Are you telling me that this document which I have in my hands, written... let me see... over three years ago and bearing your name at the bottom, was actually written by somebody else?'

'Ah, now, wai' minnit.' There was a pause for turgid, suety thought. 'Yeah. I'll send somebody up to pick it up. Take a look at it.'

'No,' replied Mutcer. 'You come up here and see it yourself. It's important.'

While the chief of Security wheezed his way up to the first floor (20 agonizing stairs; this was getting to be a habit) Mutcer had plenty of time to scatter the papers around, rub them over the ass of his pants, and stuff them casually into an old manila folder. Artificial ageing.

'Here it is. This is the original and it's not signed.'

He handed the pages to the puffing hulk across his desk and sat back to await results.

Limace cast his piggy eyes over the document. He fumbled with it, playing for time. What was goin' on? Pork had him by the balls. If he denied writing this thing it was proof he didn't know what was going on in his department. He couldn't remember for sure if he had told somebody else to write it. If not, who did write it? And why did Pork want it signed all of a goddam' sudden? Fishy. Nothing for it, he'd have to take the easy way out. What's a signature anyway?

He made his face show dawning comprehension as he pawed the document. He looked like a village idiot being given a penny.

'Oh, yeah, dis report! I din know you meant dis report. Sure! I din hunnerstan' which report you meant... Yeah.'

Pork shoved a pen at him and he signed under his name. Their eyes met and each exchanged stares of mutual understanding. You don't piss in my pocket, I won't piss in yours.

'Just in case you don't have a copy,' said Mutcer with ill-concealed sarcasm once the signature was applied and drying, 'we'll toddle along to the photocopier and make you one. Then you can put it safe in your filing cabinet, can't you?'

Once Limace had returned to his basement, Mutcer farted luxuriously, stretched his legs, and had a nip at his flask. A good morning's work, but not quite complete. Got to put copies in all the other files. Also have to have a word in the baldheaded coot's ear about this place being a fire hazard. Finally, a check on the architectural blueprints of the building; there are some plumbing connections that need reviewing. Then the stage would be nearly set!

Bill Anker was as fortunate as Mutcer. Having the chief curator stepping into the breach had taken the pressure off him. Then he had Doris, first daughter of the naval Ironsides, to pluck him from humiliation at the snap of her all-powerful fingers. Her timely arrival had saved him from certain self-incrimination at the hands of the police. She had seen the frantic action around the museum during *On The Spot News*, realized that it involved the moron that Daddy (the Admiral) had told her to avoid like poisoned canapés, and had rushed to the rescue.

She had driven him back home as quickly as she could. They lived across the river, only 15 minutes away, on Amanita Crescent, in one of those suburbs that have mushroomed up on the outskirts of most towns. They occupy treeless, raw spaces named after the natural features they have obliterated, such as The Pines, Quail Ridge, or Deer Run.

Theirs was a new house with a double garage at the front. Usually these houses are so similar, so vulgar and cheap and cheerful, that you are convinced that the people in them match their surroundings. All the houses around had mass-produced pressed steel carriage lamps flanking their doors, and curlicue street numbers, and names like The Laurels or Shangri-La burnt into rustic-looking bits of wood swinging on chains. Cartwheels cut in half flanked immaculate driveways, and some houses even had bloody concrete gnomes engaged in futile fishing in plastic pools.

But their house was different. It exhibited taste. The planting of bushes and shrubs, the choice of decoration, the care in colour matching of the paint on doors and window frames, all indicated denizens with sensibility. Clearly, the aesthetic played a strong role in their daily lives. Their house was an oasis of taste in a Gobi of the ghastly. They only lived there because Daddy owned most of the neighbourhood.

It was perhaps fifty percent of tenderness that had made her rush him away from the scene of his humiliation. The other fifty percent concerned the question of reputation. She was stuck with the dear fool and it was her duty, to herself and the family name, to keep him somewhat in line. Daddy had wanted her to marry Navy, of course, and although Bill was hardly Nereus, the Old Man of the Sea, he would have to do.

Doris had fallen in love. That was the problem. It was after she had rescued Bill when he had got his hand stuck in a toilet roll dispenser during a diplomatic reception at the Hilton. He had torn the thing off the wall, and she had found him staggering around outside the washrooms with this great piece of clanking stainless-steel on his hand. That was one thing; getting the cretin past all the guests and out to the hardware store for a C-clamp and hacksaw had been something else.

It was then that she had paradoxically fallen for him; *she* could be *his* Anchor. The flower of romance is a Zone Two perennial; it is hardy and will blossom almost anywhere. But now, how to nurture it to full fruition?

Bill Anker stared out of his fifth-floor office window. It was Tuesday just before noon, the day after the riot, and he had just got back to his office from police headquarters, where he had provided a statement on his activities in yesterday's fiasco. The mess had been cleared up and it all looked quite normal now. He had got off lightly.

Nobody in the museum seemed to realize that without him in charge there would have been no riot at all, merely a noisy demonstration. The panic had been so widespread and spontaneous that it was not perceived as having a particular cause. Most fortunate. Rumours as to exactly what had happened were flying around, but so far nobody was pinning any particular blame on him. Mrs Straw, Chairperson of the Board of Trustees, had just phoned and he had put on a fair imitation of an efficient, well-organized director deeply regretful of the folly of others.

It seemed as if he could relax a little and let this whole episode blow over. Time would heal. With the true optimism only the giftedly single-minded can muster, he returned to his plans for the new museum. Perhaps the extra confidence gained from not being dragged on the carpet for a dressing down by the Board of Trustees, from not being hauled over the coals by the City Police, from not being an object of ridicule to the whole staff, caused him to decide his next course of action.

The riot had given him an idea. It might provide exactly the leverage he needed. The hint of success in the future, the clear vision vouchsafed him of himself standing in the grand exhibition hall amid crowds of admirers while champagne corks popped, blinded him to all the hazards he might face, and put unaccustomed steel into his spine.

Desperate causes demand desperate solutions he thought, as he churned out at least his eighth cliché of the morning. It is probably futile to speculate how he would have felt had he known that he and Rourke Mutcer were working for the same end; at least in material terms. Probably a loose-bowelled funk.

The telephone pierced his daydreams. The voice of Charles Orville Jones, Curator of Folk Culture, burst into his thoughts. Jones was a seedy, overweight, self-promoted guru. In his younger days he had brought a form of sneering deconstruction to his field and had been in demand for a while by professional groups who found his approach refreshing and witty. Time had worn the welcome thin. He would still peer down his nose from his personal Parnassus or Olympus, smile in benign amusement at the antics of the little people, and make supercilious, God-like pronouncements. It was just a pity that when he did speak one had the impression of a huge cathedral organ being used to play very bad music.

But this was not the C.O. Jones Anker knew! The voice was almost incoherent, stammering, and very upset indeed.

'Thank God you're back at last! Robbery!' he gasped. 'Gone! *Gold and Gems*... The statuette's gone! Come quickly! To the display...'

Oh, no! Not another theft! I don't need this!

Anker dropped the phone and rushed down to the temporary exhibition space on the west side of the second floor. The lid was off the display case and the plinth was horribly bare. Jones danced from foot to foot like a little boy under extreme hydraulic pressure, while two assistant curators and a security guard Anker had never seen before looked on. Before he could say a thing, Chief Limace wheezed in and filled the space even more.

'What? Robbery?' blurted the chief of security. 'Wossgoinonere?'

Lucian Limace was in bad shape. Too much had happened since yesterday, and he was still not fully recovered from his athletic feat of climbing to the fifth floor. He wheezed purple and dripped sweat. This job was becoming a pain in the ass.

Bill Anker made a grinding effort to hold back his panic, breathed deeply while the security chief puffed into silence, and then, in a retrained manner befitting his position said, 'Tell me exactly what has happened.'

They all began to squeak away together until he shushed them with his hands. 'One at a time! One at a time! Jones, what's happened here?'

Jones breathed deeply and calmed slightly, although he still lacked almost totally the aplomb that he normally cultivated so studiously. He would never be the same again in Anker's eyes.

'The gold statuette by Nidor has been stolen. Security discovered the theft this morning,' and he cocked his thumb at the guard cowering in Limace's shadow.

'Tell me!' demanded Anker, now getting thoroughly rattled as his active imagination painted awful scenarios of the immediate future in which board members, wreathed in smoke, hauled out his nails with red-hot pliers, and Japanese owners impaled him with burning bamboo slivers.

'I opened up the doors at 10:00 and went around as we always do,' answered the guard, a late middle-aged man with conspicuous facial veins, 'and when I come to the display case, there it was, gone.'

'Gone!' echoed Jones. 'Screws undone, case lid lifted off. Just like this! Gone!'

Anker simply couldn't understand. Neither, he suspected, could the others. How could a thief enter the building, open a display case, and steal a valuable object without every bloody alarm in the building going off, and without security knowing about it? It just didn't make sense. Unless it was done under the cover of that riot...

'Who's been on duty since yesterday?' he asked Limace.

Of course, Limace didn't have a goddamned clue, but he was hardly likely to admit it.

'You,' he commanded the guard. 'Who did you replace?' The guard mentioned the name of the Carpenter's friend.

'Get him here,' demanded Anker, and Limace slid off to use the phone.

'We should call the police,' offered Jones, now gaining some of his synthetically cultured attitude. 'This is an incident of major importance with which we are ill equipped to deal.'

Anker saw the sense of this, although not the syntax. But he was loath to do anything that might bring down more publicity. The riot last evening was bad enough, but to have the police back the very next day was inviting a public relations disaster. But what else could he do? And now the press would get onto it as well! Bad publicity piled on top of bad publicity. Would it never end? With great reluctance he walked to the front booth to make the call.

The last person on Earth Bill Anker wished to see marching through those same oaken front doors was the chief of police. When that worthy gentleman entered the building in the company of a sergeant and two constables, Anker wished he could literally sink through the floor, or slip a ring onto his finger and turn himself invisible. His mortification was only increased when the chief singled him out, approached him, and looking down from a considerable height, said in a voice that expressed distain and a weary acceptance of the follies of others, 'Well, what is it this time?'

As a very high cop he didn't have to show up for a mere robbery, but having been present at the ridiculous fiasco of the previous day, and having heard details of the earlier thefts, his interest was piqued in spite of his outward pose of studied boredom. He'd had the museum flagged in the police database, so he would be alerted when there was activity on the file.

Highly unlikely place for criminals to hang their shingles!

Anker explained the discovery of the theft, with gabbled input from the others, and showed the police the scene of the crime. When he actually used the words 'scene of the crime' the chief rolled his eyes to heaven and the sergeant grinned behind his notepad.

'All right,' announced the chief when he had seen enough, 'close the gallery, put somebody on guard here—you'll do (to one of the constables)—and get the lab boys in here. Chance of prints is remote; probably a mess, but you never know. Meanwhile, all those who know anything about this had better help us get something down on paper.'

The security guard who had made the discovery came forward and started to tell his story again, but the chief cut him off.

'All right, all right! This is obviously going to be a long one. Anywhere we can camp out for the day?' he asked in Anker's direction.

They were shown to an empty office close to Mutcer's lair near the loading bay. The chief dismissed everybody except the night guard, and told them all not to leave the building, and to hold themselves ready to be interviewed.

The constable stayed outside in the corridor while the chief went in with the sergeant and rearranged furniture to produce a makeshift inquisition chamber. Just a pity there wasn't a desk lamp they could angle towards their victims; only cold, anemic fluorescents overhead.

The security guard from the day before showed up, and was shown to the office. 'All right, wait out there, you'll be next,' barked the chief before slamming the door of the office.

The chief sat the night security guard across the table from him and explained the procedures.

'And this is Sergeant Delios. He's going to take notes. Not a statement or anything that official yet. Just notes.'

Fred Delios sat on a chair near the door and began to write. He was a man of medium build with a round, unassuming face. Out of his uniform, you wouldn't really notice him. But he hadn't become a sergeant for nothing. He was quick on the uptake, very retentive of details, good in tight corners, and not afraid to put the old boot in the balls when required. All in all, a good man to have around.

The guard was unable to add much to what he had already said, but he was adamant that nobody had entered or left the building on his shift, and that the alarms had been turned on the whole time.

The truth was actually very different. In fact, that night, as every night, there was no security guard anywhere near the displays. It was the habit of the guards to gather in the rear loading bay security booth after the museum had been closed and the late straggling workers had departed. The duty guard would do his rounds, as per the prescribed routine, switching off lights and locking doors, before joining his three companions in the back over their first case of 24 beers. This was the legacy of Limace's tribute to efficiency, although if he had ever stayed late and stumbled on them by accident, chances are the second 24 would be half finished in record time. Their boozy nights were a secret nobody would ever tell. The guards were a closed cabal.

Once as much information as possible had been extracted, the night man was shown out, and the man of the day before took his place. He moved lightly into the room; an active, younger man, not at all typical of the usual building security model, who were often older ex-servicemen. His testimony was much more interesting, and it took some time to relate and absorb.

'So then, when all hell breaks loose, you're not exactly looking after the shop, are you? I mean, here's a riot with protesters and what-not, and there you are with a plastic musket on your shoulder. Did you check the displays when things got back to what might be described as normal?'

'Well, no. It was late, eh? And I was helping clean up. Guard shift changed at nine.'

This was getting uncomfortable. He had let his pal the Carpenter into the building away before then; the statuette was gone by 8:30, and he hadn't mentioned Easel's afternoon visit yet. The cop was beginning to tread horribly close. Soon it would all have to come out.

'So the museum's closed on Mondays? Nobody in the galleries? Before the riot, or after when it all calms down?'

'Yes, that's right.'

'No activity that you might regard as suspicious? Have I got that right?'

'Suspicious? No.' *Oh, Jesu! Now he's beginning to tread real close again!*

'So, you're all alone in the booth for your shift, and nobody goes in or out while you're there?'

The guard squirmed under his gaze. He was getting sucked deeper and deeper into a pit of lies. No backing out now; he was too far in. *But this is worse than lying to that son of a bitch Easel; this was friggin' perjury!* He was scared and wished he had never got sucked in at all. The more the chief stared, the more he fidgeted.

'So, what do they do when you start an eight-hour shift then?'

64

asked the cop. 'Put in a catheter? Or do they give you a pisspot under the desk? Or perhaps you've got a bladder the size of a black garbage bag?'

'Oh, sure, put it like that. Yeah, we're not there all the time. I mean, breaks and that.'

'So, somebody could have sneaked in while you were taking a leak or whatever?'

'Yeah, sure, but it's only for a minute or two...'

He was right, the chief thought, there wouldn't be time to get in and out. This was useless.

'Until the demo, then, nobody disturbed your tranquility? No suspicious activity in or out of your door?' The chief sat in thought for an uncomfortably long time. 'Just you and an empty building...' he mused, staring at him and exuding suspicion like the fog from an ultrasonic humidifier. When he was thinking he would gnaw at the side of a large, accusatory forefinger. He did this now, oblivious.

Here came the horrible moment. The guard steeled himself. *I've got to look innocent. Slow the old heart rate.* 'No, nobody, except Mr Easel, of course, but he's not suspicious...'

'Easel? Who's Easel?' cut in the chief.

'Just Easel. Mr Easel, the guy in charge of Conservation.'

'And he was in the building? How long for? When?'

'Dunno. He didn't stop at the booth. Didn't talk to me. Ten minutes, maybe.'

There! He had done it! It was a relief to have said it, but it was a bit like the relief of finally letting go of a branch when you're hanging above a ravine.

'What time was this?' demanded the chief, slightly losing his air of detachment.

'About three, I suppose. Sorry, I didn't think it was important.'

'Well, maybe it was, and maybe it wasn't, but you might have remembered sooner, and saved me some time. Around three o'clock? In and out in 10 minutes?'

'Yes.'

The chief of police said nothing, but stared disconcertingly at the guard. Finally, the tension broke. 'Okay, you can go.' He showed him out of the door.

'You,' he said to the constable in the corridor. 'Find this guy Easel and get him here pronto! And for Christ's sake find me some coffee!'

This request was a huge mistake.

The museum staff's coffee machine was tolerated, but not loved. The machine itself—a piece of high-tech wizardry with its lights and ubiquitous beepers—ground and filtered the beans before your very eyes. Having remembered to place a cup under its nether nozzle, the customer was rewarded with a splattering micturition of perhaps the worst coffee achievable without recourse to a jar of instant, freeze-dried powder. The bonus of having the beans ground before your very eyes was offset by the fact that they were of the lowest quality obtainable, and by the fact that the entire mechanism was coated with rancid, bitter coffee oils, baked on. But it is a remarkable fact of human nature that people will gladly tolerate the insufferable if it provides a quick shot of caffeine.

While waiting for Easel to appear the chief was discovering that museum coffee and police headquarters coffee had an awful lot in common; awful.

After some 15 or 20 minutes, Easel presented himself at the door of the office.

'Come in, sit down.'

Woodrow Wilson Easel had had a lot of time to think things over while he was making his way from Building Four. *What the hell do the cops want with me? And just a day after the incident with the loose screws.* The more he thought about those loose screws, the more suspicious he got. He had obviously stumbled on a failed burglary attempt. But how was that guard involved? You don't just find some screws on the floor, just like that. But if he was abetting a thief, he would hardly make a big deal of the screws. It didn't add up, unless the guy was innocent. But he didn't want him innocent; he was friends with that fuckin' carpenter. Easel's dislikes often coloured his opinions, and so he construed motives and actions based upon what he felt about people, rather than what logic dictated. For all his apparent self-control, he was actually a mess of conflicting emotions beneath that controlling, callous exterior. Imagine a super-hard coconut filled with rancid milk, or a very deep well with a small child crying inaudibly at the bottom.

'Sit down please. First off, you may not have heard so I'd better tell you. A gold statuette has been stolen from the displays. Had you heard?'

Easel kept control of his face and thought hard. *Holy shit! This is even more suspicious than I thought. That guard! I knew he was hiding something, and I bet he's teamed up with some thief, just like I thought.*

But then why call me? Doesn't make any sense. Wait! Jesus H. Christ! They're trying to frame me! That's what they're doing! And I'll bet it's that goddam' fuckin' carpenter at the bottom of this. Jesus! Okay, keep cool; keep calm. Time to play this one real cagey.

'Stolen? No! Not the gold statuette in *Gold and Gems?*'

'The same. And whoever did it, knew how to dismantle the display cases. Takes a special screwdriver, I hear. Tell me about the special screwdriver. Not an everyday one, is it?'

'No, we made them special in our workshop. Two prongs; fixed distance, different diameters. Security precaution.'

'So how many are there? Display technicians, curators, they all have them, eh?'

'No,' replied Easel with a hint of smugness. 'On'y us. Anybody else wants access, they have to sign one out from us. There's only two. You've seen these people,' he continued smoothly. 'Would you trust them with security? No, it's gotta be placed on an intelligent and responsible footing. We're the only possible department.'

The sergeant on his chair by the door smiled and nodded as he took notes. He had seen some of the other museum staff, and he agreed wholeheartedly. Very perceptive of Mr Easel. Hit the nail right on the head.

'So the thief would have to borrow one of yours, or make a copy. Have I got that right?'

'Yeah, that's right. But we keep 'em well-guarded.'

'When was the last time you used one of them?' asked the chief, all innocence.

Easel maintained his composure and thought hard again. *Can't trip me up that easy. That security bastard! Do I spill the works about what happened yesterday and risk getting in the shit if he's already blabbed, or do I shut up and hope it hasn't come out? The way this cop's behaving, he knows about yesterday already.* He weighed the pros and cons swiftly in his mind, and decided to lay out the whole story. He slipped easily into his smooth, obliging persona and explained carefully and cooperatively how the loose screws had been discovered, and how the security guard had called him over to the museum. He had put the screws back and left the building; what else was there to say, and was there anything else he could help them with? He was all charm and courtesy.

The chief was dumbfounded, although he didn't let it show. Two utterly different stories here, and both retailers appeared equally convincing. One of these people was a gifted and persuasive liar; Easel or the security guard? He decided to draw Easel out a little. You never knew what gold and gems you could elicit if you matched courtesy for courtesy.

'So, Mr Easel, tell me; what's your view?'

'Simple. Somebody was doing the heist and got innerrupted. Then, under cover of the riot they come back and finish the job. Security musta seen him, so he's in on it too,' he replied, deflecting suspicion away from himself and onto the security guard.

This was so inconsistent that the chief felt he had to lead him a little by pointing out the gaping hole in his theory.

'If that's the case, why would he phone you? Wouldn't he just let the thief carry on?'

Easel fixed the chief with his best stare, and turned on the charm that always worked so well for him.

'I seriously think they're tryin' to frame me. Draw suspicion away from themselves. That guard; he's hiding somethin'. I can tell. That man is guilty, bee-lee-me. And they're out to get me, the whole lot of them.'

And almost—as convincing and persuasive as he was—they could indeed believe him. Delios nodded in agreement from his chair by the door, and even the chief showed some sign of credulity. However, he hadn't been a cop for all these years without learning something about criminal minds. He sat back, drew in a deep breath, and took a mouthful of cold, dark, bitter coffee. He wasn't to be drawn in that easily.

'Thank you, Mr Easel,' he almost sighed. 'You have been very cooperative.'

It hadn't taken long for Anker to tell them all he knew. As he left the office on the first floor, he encountered Rourke Mutcer going in the opposite direction. Mutcer's so sensitive but very directional nose had detected a scandal. He was on the point of stopping Anker, but the latter brushed him off and hastened to his office. He hadn't been there a few minutes before the man himself knocked on the door, stepped in without waiting to be asked, and perched one buttock on the corner of his desk, as he always did, because he knew how annoying it was. Sometimes he even knocked insolently on the inside of the door after he had entered. The room was invaded by a zephyr of rancid pork.

'Come in,' said Anker with as much irony as he could muster as Mutcer cheeked onto the desk. He was expecting to be grilled about the theft or cross-examined about the riot. He was caught flatfooted when neither of these topics was raised.

'Were you aware of the fact that this place is a fire trap? We were damned lucky that nothing caught during that, ah, unfortunate incident yesterday. I've always said this place was doomed, but people just don't seem to listen.'

'Have you? I mean, said that?' answered Anker warily. His shit-on-the-horizon radar was showing a blip.

'Of course. I've written memos, talked to people. Loosh'n Limace even did a report on it years ago.'

The signed original of which, he continued to himself, will find its way into your filing cabinet tonight. Copies to file! Ha, ha! He was thorough; very thorough. In order to make his fabrication convincing he would place a hard copy in the central file in Registry, and also update the computer records accordingly. Unknown to him, Conservation Chief Easel checked the database regularly and noted all data entry activity on files under the Conservation Department's wide jurisdiction. This included security. A few days later Easel would note on his display the addition of a file on fire safety, check out the hard copy in Registry, find it backdated, and be truly delighted. He knew Limace couldn't write, he had never seen this document before, and he noted the electronic identity of the person who had done the data entry. Mutcer! Yes, Mutcer was busy taking his good advice to heart. The subtle, scheming bastard was indeed a very good tool.

'Report?' answered Anker. 'Are you sure? I've never seen it.'

'Of course I'm sure. This place is a firetrap. And you, of all people, should know that,' he concluded nastily as Anker's eyes shifted away. 'Know what I mean?'

Anker looked like a rabbit contemplating a moving steamroller, except that rabbits are not as bald as eggs, steamrollers are not chief curators of museums, and steam propulsion has been almost entirely superseded by internal combustion for propelling road maintenance machinery. Aside from these minor considerations, the simile is fairly apt.

'Know what I mean?' repeated Pork. 'And, between you and me, there's a ton of stuff down on paper; reports, memos, notes to file...' and he lifted his cheek from the corner of the desk, opened the door and glided smoothly out of the office. He left only a miasma.

Bill Anker knew exactly what he meant. The smelly toad had used that lever before and if he ever carried through with it he, Anker, would be ruined. Finished. Damn! Damn the man! What does he want? He recalled briefly the hideous and sudden flames, the panic and terror, a ruined museum piece, his own inaction. He shoved the thoughts to the back of his mind. That was years ago! It should be past and done with. Why bring it all back now? Damn him! What does he want?

The new museum dreams had gone now; driven away totally. He went back to the window and stared. It would be good to get away to the annual museum conference out west later this week. Leave this nest of vipers for a few days anyway...

The varnish on one corner of his desk was stripped right to the bare wood. Some unaccountable chemical reaction.

CHAPTER NINE

O n Wednesday morning the chief executive of the WeWho Arts Council sat behind his desk working on a letter to the prime minister. John Indoda Enhle used a large, fat fountain pen, the colourful wooden parts of which he had turned himself on a small lathe. He wrote in a beautiful mannered hand. No recipient would ever see the handwritten work—it would be word-processed by his staff to take all the humanity out of it—but he thought better with a pen in his hand. Sure, he could use a keyboard as quickly and efficiently as anyone else, but for this kind of work there was a fine communication between paper and ink and nib and hand that brought out the best in him. The aesthetic was very important to him. The programs of the WeWho Arts Council emphasized the cultural, as opposed to the more well-publicized political, concerns of his people.

He finished his letter and sat a moment in thought. Such a long way from Treaty Bluff to this richly decorated office in the State Capital, but hard won all the way. His father had seen the worst of things, but he had encouraged his sons—John and his brother James—to think larger and wider than their sequestered territory, and it was with the current generation that such aspirations started to be possible. His father was wonderfully eccentric and told the craziest tales about life in his time, and the years before. Oh, the stories he could have told these curators and museum officials, but sleeping dogs...

There came a point some time in his teens—he couldn't recall exactly the month or even the season—when John knew he had turned a sharp corner. So many of his friends at school were destined for nothing at all, but he had realized a difference in himself. He had worked hard from that point, academically and in the community.

He wanted out badly, and for him the only way out was up. He had won a university scholarship, and that was back when people like him just didn't do that. Even so, convincing himself that he could go through and graduate had been nowhere near as hard as convincing the people who gave out the awards and honours. But he had battled through, studying law and getting called to the Bar as quite a young man. His kid brother had been deeply influenced by

71

his older sibling's success. Since he was tiny, he had looked up to his big brother and tried to emulate him, and although he didn't have the academic mind, he had gone to art school and become a highly regarded sculptor in wood. It was his kid brother's commercial success that caused Indoda Enhle to bend his own career towards the arts and culture of the WeWho. After all, second-class citizens they may still be, but their artworks were prized.

All through his academic years John Indoda Enhle had been building networks of people with influence, or those destined to wield it. He met politicians, local leaders, religious and spiritual heads, press moguls and captains of industry, all the time impressing them with his credentials and laying the groundwork for the future. He knew politics, he knew people, and he could play one against the other like a fine musical instrument. He had been a lawyer, an activist, a social worker, and a politician. And for much of the last decade he had been a non-government organization wheeler and dealer, working on the inside, dealing with the aesthetic rather than the political. Not bad for a kid from the outside, and not yet seeing forty-five.

He had had much criticism from some of his own people over his choice to work with, and not against, the suits, but he had stuck to his guns. And his pens. He argued that protests, strikes, and the other actions painted negative images of the WeWho. He always pushed the positive. Now, as chief executive of this Arts Council, he looked people straight in the eye. It had been won the hard way, within the system through powerful political will, intensive lobbying, and lots of hard work.

Such a sadness that Dad hadn't lived to see it all... Still, my success is his legacy...

This garbage around the Museum of Personkind two days ago did more harm than good, in his estimation. Fortunately, no group of his people had had anything to do with it, as he had taken pains to point out to the press. Even so, that particular collection—the focus of the protest—was a nasty can of worms, and it made him uneasy thinking about it. His past kept tapping him on the shoulder. He kept hearing Dad's voice.

'Your visitor is here, sir,' peeped the intercom.

'Thank you, Gloria. Send him in.' He sheathed his fat fountain pen and put it carefully into his top pocket.

Anker entered the office with a little trepidation. It had taken quite a lot of courage to make the appointment, and quite a bit of subterfuge to escape notice as he left the museum. He was sure he hadn't been spotted. His head would be on the block if the chairperson of the Board found out. The Board didn't act often, but this would really give them a prod. The chair didn't like having her arms, or any other parts of her, twisted. He'd danced with Lana Straw once at a reception; he knew.

'Ah, it's very good of you to see me, Mr er... ah, Enhle.'

'Indoda Enhle. Two words,' he replied laconically.

'Indoda? Ah, good. Right. Indoda Enhle. Yes. Er... You'll probably have heard about the demonstration at the museum, day before yesterday?' He paused. 'Yes, of course you would. Being a WeWho, and... and...'

Indoda Enhle sat and marinated in silence. Anker stumbled on.

'Yes, well, get to the point, eh?... They want us to give the stuff back to you people. Treaty Bluff. But you'll agree the artifacts are better off where they are. Custodians. Looking after the... Ah, I... I mean we... we need a new museum. To house all the valuable treasures, you know. And you people have a sort of vestibule interest, if you get my meaning. Lots of your stuff in there... Ha, ha! And a powerful lobby. You could help us. Benefit for all of us in the long run...'

Bill Anker ran down and stopped.

Indoda Enhle sat wooden faced for a few seconds. The sheer bald-headed effrontery of it took his breath away. It was unbelievable that anybody could be so naïve as to think that the Arts Council would even stoop to recognize those parasites who had laid siege to the museum, let alone deign to align itself against them? The nerve! However, he had not achieved his present position by betraying his feelings to every lunatic he had to deal with. And, as he had dealings with the museum's ethnologists and archaeologists, it would be well to maintain cordial relationships. But this second encounter with their director was not all that impressive. He maintained his composure with an almost tangible effort.

'The issue of repatriation is certainly one that has been on the minds of many of my people. It would behoove the museum to concentrate more than it has to date upon the issue, and any input into the consequent decision-making structure that we might provide could be a point of discussion at our next council meeting.'

'Well, thank you. We have a committee to look into a pogrom of repatriation, but... early days yet... not much to report...'

'Thank you so much for bringing this matter to my attention. As to support for a new museum, the matter of whether the material is better cared for where it is, as opposed to returning it to its erstwhile owners, is a complex one. I cannot, at this point in time, give you a definitive answer, but I can assure you that the matter will receive attention when next my colleagues meet. Good morning Mr Anker.'

The absolute, baldheaded nerve of it! But even though the little bastard was pitifully naive, he might just get what he wanted. Funnily enough, Indoda Enhle's term on the board of trustees some years ago, and his associations with other professional staff, had softened him to the museum. If he had his way things would be very different. And maybe it *was* time to start wielding a little influence in the right places? After all, he was on more than nodding terms with Anker's father-in-law, and there was a source of ready money, if you like!

Well, you never knew...

Anker returned to his office somewhat chastened. He had the impression that his proposal had not met with as much warmth as it could. He realized that he hadn't stated his case well, but even so... Perhaps the Public Service had courses you could take on assertiveness and maintaining a working dialogue? He'd have to look into it. He sighed and picked up the Styrofoam cup of coffee he had just coaxed out of the machine in the staff room. He swallowed and shuddered. God, it was awful!

Draining the last drop of nectar and plopping the cup into his waste bin, Anker took up the report he had found filed under 'fire,' just where Pork had hinted it was. He was sure he had never seen it before.

'Inasmuch as the building may be considered as two separate entities' (he read) 'conjoined by the central foyer, it can be argued that a destructive fire, originating in a discrete location, could be confined to one half of the building, the other being effectively insulated and isolated by the fire gap of the foyer...'

Limace wrote this?

'Whereas a grave risk obtains throughout the edifice...' Obtains? Edifice? Limace? He must have accidentally read a book!

'Easy accessibility of sprinkler system shut-off valves on the fifth floor, and the ready flammability of both structure and contents...' Loosh'n Limace *wrote this?!*

He was now certain he had never seen the report before, but

74

there it was, signed and dated, apparently genuine. At the bottom was the subscript: cc. Chief Curator, Admin. Officer, Museum Security, Central File.' He had checked; the copies existed in the other files. A security guard—the young new guy—had kindly gone through Limace's files and retrieved their copy for him. Also in his own file were two old memos from Mutcer, both urging immediate action on fire safety procedures. He'd swear he'd never seen those before either. He put the report back into its dog-eared folder.

What the hell was going on? It was all very ominous. He felt control slipping from him. And for one who has so little, this is a doubly unpleasant sensation.

The *Duke of Clarence* pub (or *The Puke* as its regulars called it) was a favourite watering hole of the museum crowd. It was the sort of place that appealed to them. It had the old world charm of beams on the ceiling (made of resin and fiberglass, naturally), mirrors with ads for Guinness and Rickard's Red, a jar of pickled eggs on the counter that no one in living memory had dared sample, and of course lots of old woodwork, suitably stained and battered. The hum of conversation and the clink and clatter of glasses were punctuated by the dull thud of darts, or the ponk when somebody hit a wire. The landlord, as he liked to style himself, had resolutely resisted gambling machines, and that was good. Inevitably, there was a television hanging over the bar, tuned to a sports channel but with the sound pleasantly muted. A recent citywide ban on smoking in public places had quite paradoxically spoiled the atmosphere of the place, but at least you could see from one side to the other. All in all, a great place to be.

The booths along the wall furthest from the window were fairly secluded. Two people with connections to the museum were having a little tête-à-tête over a few beers, and it was important not to be overheard. They were discussing the heist, a couple of nights ago, of the gold statuette from its display case in the *Gold and Gems* exhibit.

'A perfect set-up for our mutual friend, I must say! You handled that really well. Get the bastard to visit the display with his little screwdriver, get 'im on video, then I sneak in the same night and pinch the statuette. And that friggin' riot! What a way to distract attention! Couldn't have done it better if it had been planned.' He took a pull at his beer. 'You are still with me, aren't you?'

'Yes, yes! I told you, I hate that shit Easel! And he hates me, but this is all too scary. The police scared the crap out of me in that

75

interview. You don't know what you're making me do! It's not just petty theft, y'know. That statue's worth thousands. It's a jail sentence, for Christ's sake!'

He reached into an inner pocket. 'Anyway, here's your friggin' screwdriver. If I got caught with this I'd be dead meat!'

'Thanks. I'll hang onto this little homemade jobbie. Never know when it might be handy again.'

He tucked it quickly into his bag.

'But that's bullshit about a jail sentence!' he continued. 'It's only a friggin' statue, for pete's sake!'

'You're not getting it, are you? It isn't "just a friggin' statue". It's some Japanese treasure or something, and the shit's hitting the fan internationally.'

'You what?'

'Limace was hauled up by the management. They told him that our Ambassador was called in by the Japanese government to explain what happened, and what's being done about it. It's a big deal with them! Just a friggin' statue…? Yeah, right!'

'Hoo… Suddenly the game's gone up a notch.'

The Carpenter was lost in thought for a moment. Shee-it. Japanese government making waves. Crap flying in high places. Haven't bitten off too much, have I? Ah well, hung for a sheep…

'So, how did it go with the video surveillance after I left?'

'Fine. The tape shows him pissing about with the case, and then there's a view of the case empty. Looks like a perfect sequence, only it's hours apart. Took the second one around 8:30.'

'Foolproof?'

'Yeah. I'm good at this stuff, man! There's no time record. Just random sequences. People who bought that gear were cheapskates. Believe me, it's my business!'

'You've done a great job! Drink up!'

The Guard swallowed half his beer and sighed. 'After what he's done to people… Shit! After what he's done to you! He deserves all he gets. But…'

'He soured Stephanie on me, too. Did you know that?'

'Bastard! Give her one his little talks, did he? Like I say, he deserves all he gets. But…'

'But what?'

'Well, you been stealing all sorts of stuff off of other people this last month. Ever since you got sacked. Purses and that. I don't see how stealing other people's stuff gets back at him.'

'You'll have to be patient. I know what I'm doing. And they're all going to get their stuff back anyways.'

'What? How? I just don't get it!'

'And I'm not going to explain right now. I just know what I'm doing, that's all.'

'I can't keep letting you in like this. People are going to notice that stuff's getting stolen on my shift. That cop! And this shit with Japan. It's too dangerous.'

The Carpenter took a huge mouthful of beer, swallowed deeply, and crammed in a handful of pretzels. 'Jush wunsh more. Thash all I need,' he crunched through crushed pretzels. 'C'mon, just once.'

'I've got to think about this. When you pinched the statue I thought I was for it. That was too much. I mean, small stuff from people's lockers and that, maybe… I dunno. But that statue! I'm lucky to still have a job, no thanks to you.'

'What? Limace on your case?'

'Yeah, shit rolls downhill! God, I'd like to see the back of him! I could do his job in my sleep. Same way he does it!'

They laughed and drank more beer.

'But it's for a good cause. This whole thing,' said the Carpenter. 'You know that, don't you?'

'I don't know nothing anymore,' replied the Guard. 'I hate that asshole Easel and I hate that asshole Limace. That's all I know.'

'So you'll do it?'

'Well, I dunno. I've got to think about my future. I'm getting sucked in and I'm scared! This is your fight, not mine.'

'All right. Think. I'll let it cool off for a while. Talk to you again in a week.'

They ordered another round, drank deeply, and swore damnation to their mutual friends.

CHAPTER TEN

The introduction of economical desktop computers had unleashed a tsunami of information technology that had overwhelmed the museum, as it had so many other organizations, transforming their *modi operandi* in profound and permanent ways. Much of the neglect by the curatorial staff of the displays and the objects in storage could be blamed on the enormous slices of time that the computer carved from their daily work schedules (in addition to the pall of distrust and watchfulness that Easel had cast over their handling of historic objects). Far from being the labour-saving device it was touted to be, the computer actually lurked on everybody's desk like an enthralling toad, and made increasing demands of their time and attention. The fact that free solitaire and ping-pong games came with some of their software packages didn't help.

In no other organization could it have been more obvious that the paperless office was the most uproarious joke of the 20th century. As computers proliferated towards the enviable goal of one on every desk and a few spare, consumption of paper skyrocketed. Vast wooden pallets carrying hundreds of packages of paper were forklifted into the museum's administration section every month. Stands of trees, forested hillsides and shady dells were swept clean, pulped, bleached, spread thin, trimmed and packaged so that the administrators, the savants, the editors and the authors could make dot-matrix printers and photocopiers red hot with their copious jottings.

This electronic landslide coincided nicely with the museum's structural reorganization, so that not only was there a requirement for documents on the widest range of museum policies and practices, there was also the capability to churn them out *en masse*. Far from rendering filing cabinets obsolete, the computer stimulated the redoubled manufacture of these supposedly historic pieces of office furniture. The agèd floors of the main museum building groaned under the load.

All the museum's computer systems were serviced and maintained by two pimply youths scarcely out of their teens. Every sentence they spoke was punctuated with 'like' and concluded with 'and stuff.' They were arrogant little swine who should really have been playing

78

Atari war games in their mothers' basements, while every nuance of their illiteracy was laid open like wounds upon society, their corporeal reality hidden behind electrons and photons. Instead, they were employed by the museum to service, jury-rig and debug the many electronic systems. While their genius with electronics went without saying, they had limited social skills, having much more satisfying intercourse with motherboards than with mother nature. Their hardware had never entered anyone else's software. This lack of empathy spilled over into their daily dealings. With the museum staff—their clients—they were brusque, condescending and impatient. And there are always those well-meaning people who don't cotton to computers all that well, and who are forever asking questions which, from a technical point of view, may seem very stupid. After all, they were the clients.

But the techies didn't set up the system, so it was unfair to give them a hard time over it. In the usual Museum of Personkind fashion, money was saved by co-opting in-house IT 'expertise.' Databases were a relatively new thing, and while you could buy software off the shelf, there was this benign but whacked-out idea that some few staff knew what all other staff needed. Bill Anker had just recently had the awful experience of in-house 'expertise' in his catastrophic survey of the museum's inadequate and multifarious buildings. In retrospect, perhaps this debacle had taught him something, but it was, of course, too late for the museum's highly ramified and all invasive computer network, which had been recently installed.

Dr Prakeesh had been put in charge of devising the system on the mistaken assumption that his expertise was in some way comparable to that available in the real world for enormous fees per hour. Sunil Prakeesh was from the Indian subcontinent, although he had come here many years ago. He was a dear old soul. He must have been in his late 50s, but he always gave an even more grandfatherly impression. People with personal troubles would find their way to his comfortably cluttered office-cum-laboratory in the basement of the west wing of the main museum building.

Archaeological specimens, books and piles of paper were heaped and scattered in what he himself described as patterns of deterministic chaos. A stuffed bird maintained sentry duty on all who came in through the door from the vantage point of a tall, old bookcase. Tea making equipment of startling complexity dominated the desk. He was fond of white tea and made it fresh in a kerosene-heated samovar.

Whatever old Prakeesh might be doing, if someone dropped in he would lay it gently aside, push his small round glasses onto his forehead, rub his eyes with his knuckles, and sit back almost horizontally in an old wooden chair to listen attentively to every word. Nobody was ever sure whether he had given them good advice, or indeed if he had said anything much at all, but it just felt good to lay out one's heart to a resonant, sympathetic fellow traveler. Boyfriend troubles, anxieties of work and home, and sour financial dealings all acquired realistic perspective under his benign influence. Interactions with Easel occupied a considerable portion of his 'counselling,' although nothing went beyond the walls of his office.

He had been playing with computers on and off for years. He still possessed his first, a Sinclair ZX-81, now a true museum piece. He had begun seriously using the computer as a tool in the Commodore 64 days, and while his knowledge had progressed, it remained deeply sequestered in his own specialty, the manufacture of hand tools out of obsidian, a hard glassy mineral much used by early Man. His data-base, World Obsidian Tools Integrated Survey and Inventory Tracker (WOTISIT), was the talk of the paleoarchaeology circuit in these days when databases were still in their infancy.

So Sunil was tasked with bringing the museum into the computer age. The trouble was that within the world of the museum his isolated tinkering was assumed to be real-world capability, and this did rather go to his head. So he tried out of kindness to create a system that would do everything for everybody, and ended up with one that did very little for everybody, or almost everything for nobody. It was rather callous of the museum to allow him to go this far unchecked.

He was limited in his designs by the software chosen for the task. A committee had been struck, and after only one meeting a software rep had sold them a package for a price just too good to miss. It turned out later that he was somebody's friend, although everyone on the committee disavowed the connection. Because Prakeesh liked acronyms he called his system ARTS, for Artifact and Research Retrieval System. Once the staff began to use it however, in honour of its predecessor WOTISIT, they secretly and rather unkindly named it FUKNOSE.

The all-encompassing business processes system did work, as far as the lame software would let it, but from its inception it was clearly not up to the task. It was slow, Byzantine and inconsistent.

It was not user-transparent, as they say.

And it crashed frequently.

But most of all, its structure provided an insight into the mind of its designer, and this is never flattering. On the practical level of making the thing do what you wanted, there was just too much to know for the average, non-computer literate staff member. And that was most of them.

Because the two pimply techies had not been involved with building the system, they had no interest in its general utility. So, the larger picture was invisible to them. The relative convenience or inconvenience of using the system as a whole had little relevance in comparison with the efficient functioning of its individual components. (A question of not being able to see the forest for the clear-cutting machinery.)

This electronic balls-up was, sad to say, another legacy of the Bill Anker who was surrounded by jesters and knaves, and was driven through his weakness whither their agendas or their ignorance sent him.

Getting the museum's collections on line was a continuation of the nightmare. Since Dr Prakeesh had built his unique and idiosyncratic system for stone tools, database development had come a long way. He had started at a time when databases were in their infancy and he had used as his basic software a hierarchical program. It worked adequately but relational databases were beginning to transform the way that data were stored and retrieved. Systems like WOTISIT were becoming out of date, and simply incompatible with later applications.

Bill Anker had all this explained to him by a consultant of the Unified Collections Entity. The two were meeting for lunch on Thursday, four days after the riot and robbery, in a small, comfortable restaurant not far from the museum. Anker had chosen *Squids Inc.* in the old market area, because he enjoyed seafood, and it was very quiet and offered a passable list of wines.

UNCLE was a federally based organization that was doing a round-the-country blitz, trying to get museums up to speed electronically, and offering financial inducements. The consultant was a man of medium height, impeccably dressed in a three-piece, and sporting a watch that was obviously made to give others status-based information, rather than telling the wearer the time. He smelled of something expensive and not very masculine. He was just a little too smooth by half. This man from UNCLE had an annoying habit of continually rearranging the tableware into symmetrical patterns, making microscopic adjustments to alignments so that the relationships of knives, forks, spoons and cruets were just so.

They ate first and talked around a range of museum issues. Dessert over, they got down to business. The consultant aligned the edge of his napkin with the place mat, moved his unused coffee spoon three degrees to the north, and commenced.

'See, there are your hierarchical, your network, and your relational models. Now, just about everybody these days is using relational databases. And that's your problem 'cuz you've used an out-of-date model.'

'So, the museum's artifact databases can't be included in the national program as they stand?'

'Exactly. Basically, you've got this old guy... Brackish? That right?'

'Prakeesh. Dr Sunil Prakeesh.'

'Yeah, well, when he put together his WOTISIT he used a pretty old platform.'

'Platform?' asked Anker, thinking of... well... platforms. Lecture, concert, graduation, bus station.

'Your software.'

'Oh, I see. So a platform is a software, is it? Funny. I've always thought of platforms as quite hard.'

The man from UNCLE sighed and moved a fork with micrometric precision. 'You went with a very out-of-date software, is what I'm saying.'

'Well, there were economies, of course, and we did get a good deal on it.'

He remembered the meeting with the software consultant and some of the other more technical of his staff members—including Easel, now he thought of it—when they were planning the system. It was pretty clear that the team he had assembled had been sold a dog, while the members were far from competent enough to take such sweeping and far-reaching decisions. Sunil was a nice person—very well meaning—but maybe he wasn't God's gift to IT after all.

'Yep. Software companies are always unloading all sorts of stuff as it goes out of date. These good deals are never as good as they look! Bet your tech boys can't even get training on it.'

'How did you know that?'

'Stands to reason. Old software, lots of new stuff on the market.

Could you find driving lessons for a steam tractor in the Yellow Pages?'

Anker conceded that such lessons might not be all that easily available by letting his fingers do the walking. But it still begged the big question: what to do?

'Scrap it,' replied the systems man with a long swig at his glass of white Domaine d'Iesel. 'Pull the plug, because your problems are not going to get any better.'

'But we can't scrap the system! The entire museum runs on it!'

'*What!?* Oh, fuck, no! Oops, 'scuse my mouth. But you didn't put the whole shebang on it, did you? No, no, no. UNCLE deals with the databases for the *collection*. That's my bailiwick. Migrate the data to a new platform. That's easy, and that's what we can help you with. Jeez, what you do with the entire network, LAN, tracking system, financial coding, travel, acquisitions and all the other stuff you've added on is totally somebody else's problem. And, boy, am I glad it's not mine!'

Bill sipped thoughtfully at his wine and said nothing. He felt as close to drowning as one can when sitting at a red gingham table in a seafood restaurant. High-tech-speak was beyond him at the best of times, but all this talk of scrapping had him in a complete funk. All the more reason to get out for the weekend, give his paper at the upcoming museum conference in the west of the island and, basically, throw a bit of joy and satisfaction into his life. Just couldn't wait to get on the plane tonight.

'But I'll tell you what not to do with it,' continued this irrepressible pessimist. 'Don't keep trying to fix it.'

Anker had authorized several very expensive returns from the software consultants already, and every time they 'fixed' something the staff complained that the system was just the same, if not worse. And as more data were added it was getting slower and slower. One joker had even fashioned a hopper out of cardboard and attached it to the side of his computer. Written large near the top edge was the instruction 'coal in here,' and an arrow.

'Throwing good money after bad, that is.'

Chief of Conservation Easel loved the computer system the museum had installed. He had been on the committee, and he knew a damned sight more about computers than most of the others. He had subtly steered the purchase of this stale software because he could see that a chaotic and unfriendly system would be much better to manipulate and control than one that was efficient and well balanced.

Moreover, during his stint he had made sure to be included on the passwords working group, so he knew them all. When the pimply youths came on staff, he was the first to greet them, and he took them into his confidence with backslapping bonhomie, coffee and oodles of charm. Unaccustomed as they were to human intercourse of any kind, they took to him like shit to Velcro. They were in his pocket from the word go. Of course he collected information on them as well.

Among the favours the pimply youths did for Easel were details on password updates and changes to the structure, and access to a wide range of information that might normally be considered other people's business. The macro that allowed him to see what Mutcer was doing with the fire report—the one that could print out all activity on files under the Conservation Department's wide jurisdiction—was perhaps the most legitimate and least invasive.

But more far-reaching was Easel's brilliant takeover of data entry validation. Through his usual subtle combination of syrup and threat at the management level, he had manipulated the Conservation Department into a position of enormous power. His department, and by extension he and he alone, had the final say on what went into the databases, and under what conditions.

When data were entered by any staff member, the electronic copy was passed through him and cleared before becoming part of the permanent electronic record. Most stuff got passed without a look— it would have consumed enormous amounts of time to check everything, and it would have been a complete waste of time—but it was the principle of the thing that counted.

It is the overt fact of control, not the effectiveness with which it is wielded, that matters.

Access to the computerized systems of the entire institute promised epic dimensions of control. But the work Easel did was very subtle. Distinction between the original artifacts in storage and the copies in the displays was far too obvious electronically to his way of thinking, especially after these meddling UNCLE people had done interfering. So, his quiet Saturdays and Monday afternoons were well spent carefully and slowly altering data. And, of course, a relational database would have made this impossible.

It was Easel's mad idea that, once the museum was linked with the Unified Collections Entity, images of the copies would be on the island-wide database, while the originals would be kept safe from harm and other people's interference.

What happened to the copies in the display galleries, and who believed what about them in future, would take care of itself. That was Mutcer's little project, and good luck to him.

CHAPTER ELEVEN

C onference attendance was a necessity at the Museum of Personkind;
not just a perk. Ample money was always set aside for travel, per
diem allowance, accommodation and other expenses for as many of
the upper echelon staff as possible. Presenting papers at such
gatherings was an essential component in the academic career paths
these museum professionals followed.

There were annual meetings for the widest range of museum
specialties—curators, conservators, reproduction technicians, gift shop
staff—each of which had its own organization. There was even an
interest group within the general museum assembly just for directors
and administrators. Bill Anker had participated actively in this group
for a number of years, and he looked forward to their meetings for
months in advance.

Conferences were a bit like vacations. No, they *were* vacations.
The only work you had to do in perhaps a week—or at least a long
weekend—was to present your paper and field questions, a process
that lasted half an hour at the maximum. The rest of the time you had
free to hobnob with colleagues and friends, take in the many social
activities laid on for the occasion, and attend just enough sessions to
make it look as if you were attending more than you actually were.

Then there was the food and drink. Always copious, every bit on
the expense account or provided by the hosts, and of a quantity and
variety not normally provided in the kitchen of Amanita Crescent.

A further, and perhaps defining, feature of conferences was the
absence of your significant other. Spouses sometimes did accompany
their other halves to these functions, but unless they were also museum
professionals, or had some other touristic or personal interest, it
could be excruciatingly dull. The wiser spouses stayed at home, and
kept their fingers crossed that their loved ones would behave with
some decorum.

And there were noteworthy breaches. Liaisons at most conferences
provided grist that the mills of the museum world would grind into
rumour, only to see its flour bloom into fiction months after. It was
so easy to be naughty when you passed each other like ships in the
night. Most times it was the glimpse of a masthead light or an
illuminated cabin porthole, a mournful deep-throated horn in the

fog. So what if you occasionally came alongside amid the pack-ice, threw grapples and boarded a vessel that was hove to?

Bill Anker had never succumbed to any such temptation. He followed the wise adage of Mark Twain that 'There are several good protections against temptation, but the surest is cowardice.' The overwhelming fear of being found out provided the best prophylactic on the planet. Besides, not too many ships had him on their radar in the first place. No, he was content to watch the paths of others, to observe the tides in their fortunes, and see the sea lanes merge and diverge.

'Okay. You're sure you've got everything?'

He snapped out of his reverie. 'Yes, yes. We've checked already.'

'Well, it's worth checking again,' said Doris. 'Remember when you forgot all your slides and I had to send them by courier?'

'You've never let me forget. I have them here.' He opened his briefcase, fumbled for a panicky moment, and found the box in relief.

They were sitting in her car outside the departures gate at the airport on Thursday night. He was on his way west to the much anticipated annual museum association conference, and would fly back on Monday. It was a welcome interlude from the pressures of the job just now—the riot, the continuing robberies and the computer problems had quite shaken him—and the museum could run itself very well for a couple of days. In fact, because of the layered non-decision-making structure at present in place, the institution operated as a headless automaton at the best of times. No difference in its everyday operation would be perceptible because nothing decided at the top had any relevance to what went on at the bottom.

She gave him a peck on the cheek—nothing more in such a public place—and he got out of the car and went round to the trunk for his suitcase.

'Have a good trip. Give me a call. And don't do anything I wouldn't do!'

'Course not! Bye. See you soon,' and he disappeared through the rotating door.

Doris sat for a while in thought. Of course he wouldn't do anything. He's good. But is he good because he is innately so, or is he good because he's scared of what might happen if I found out? Sure, he has a finely developed sense of what's right and what's wrong. That's why it's so agonizing for him as a director sometimes. Complicity in the fuck-ups of others, not assertive enough to take corrective action, and without a thick rhinoceros hide to help distance himself.

On the other hand, as a director he has to be seen at all times to be maintaining high standards. Of course, having married into my lot, the bar gets even higher. And besides, there probably aren't too many who would give him a second look. So he remains good, and the circumstances and motives that drive his goodness don't really matter.

She sighed, started the car, and swung out into the traffic.

While the cat's away... Pork Mutcer chose Anker's absence to do a bit of background work in the further gestation of his master plan. He entered the front security booth of the museum on Friday morning and plonked himself down on a corner of the guard's desk. The guard had encountered Mutcer on several occasions and wasn't all that impressed. Then, last week, just as he was letting his carpenter friend into the building, he had seen him skulking around. He didn't like it. Now, encountering him again, he had a trapped expression on his face. His eyes shifted from one object to another, avoiding those of Mutcer, who was staring directly at him.

'So, what if I wanted to get in the back door one night, really late, without anybody ever knowing? How would I go about it?' he asked quietly.

'I dunno what you're talking about. You just get a pass, that's all.'

'We're not talking about passes here, my friend. And, yes, you do know what I'm talking about.'

'I can't let nobody in without a pass. That's the rules.'

'Oh, yes you can. I want in. And I don't want anybody knowing about it. Simple.'

'Nah, nah. Come on! I can't get involved in anything like that!'

'What? Suddenly all ethical and moral, are we?'

'Look, I don't know what you mean, so why don't you just get out of here. I got things to do.'

He waved the air suggestively with his hand.

'Don't know what I mean? Don't mind helping a thief to steal stuff, but you don't know what I mean? That what you're saying? Is it?'

'I told you, I don't know what you're talking about! Leave me alone!'

'All right,' hissed Mutcer, dropping all the playacting. 'You have been letting somebody into this building on a regular basis to steal stuff. I've seen it, I'll witness it, and you're as good as behind bars, so don't give me any of this crap about you don't know!'

'You liar! You're just trying to scare me! You don't know a thing!'

Mutcer mentioned the Carpenter's name, slowly and quietly. The guard's face fell. He realized he was trapped.

'How did you...'

'I know everything that goes on in this place. I saw you and him on Monday. At the front door!'

'All right, all right. What do you want?'

'I told you. I want in. And I want your help. You'll tell me how to get in, where to find the keys, and you won't say a word to anybody. Clear?'

'And you won't tell about...'

'As long as you do exactly as I tell you, it will be our little secret, won't it?'

The security guard nodded.

'But if you let one word out,' concluded Pork venomously, 'I'll break you. I will destroy you. Do you understand?'

The Guard nodded once again. It was a complete capitulation. He told him how and when to gain access to the main museum building, highlighting the weaknesses in Limace's trusty employees, and told him where to find the keys, and which key did what. All possible beans were spilled.

Mutcer left the booth and headed back to his office, another boulder in the avalanche of his treachery poised.

The guard sat back in his chair and sighed. He had taken this job on because it looked easy, for Christ's sake. All you did was sit in a chair in a booth, right? And when people came in you signed them in the book and gave them tags and stuff. So how come he was totally sucked into this stupid caper with the Carpenter? And now he was being threatened by the Head Curator. And what the hell was *he* doing, wanting to get in all sneaky at night?

Then there was the director, Anker, asking him about some fire security report in the Slug's files. The report had been easy to find because there was dick-all else in the drawer. Fishy! He was sucked right in, and he didn't like it one little bit.

He thought about Mutcer and he thought about that bastard Easel and he thought about Limace. What wouldn't I give to fix all three of them!

The conference was rewarding all of Bill Anker's expectations. The hotel was good, there were late nights of yarning and boozing with colleagues he seldom saw, and most of the papers he attended had some merit. He had made only one mistake so far by sitting in on a presentation entitled 'A Critical Analysis of Actions Taken Upon Historic Musical Instruments.' It had looked almost interesting on the program, but proved to be a tortuous set of case studies larded with obscure jargon and delivered with a grating English accent, and it also overran its time slot yet still wasn't brought to a satisfactory conclusion. And he had sat in the centre of a row, instead of on the aisle! Idiot! It made him (almost) admit that this was the price you had to pay for getting a free ride here. But apart from this little downer the conference had been great.

After the conference was over, and delegates would compare notes on the quality of the presentations from the perspectives of distance and time, it would be generally agreed that one of the better papers was in the ethnology sessions, entitled 'A Pan-Northern Stylistic Concordance: Common Motifs *A Mari Usque Ad Mare.*' (This may sound a mite pretentious, but it is about typical for gatherings of this kind.) The author argued that while pre-Western contact trading patterns across the whole island should also be extended by the academic community to include artistic styles. Thus, while distinct regional styles and choices of materials were clearly evident, a sharing of certain basic motifs and materials across distinct and geographically distant cultures was also apparent. The evidence for this thesis was rather selective, being confined to just one collection, but nevertheless well founded. Bill Anker missed this one, which is a pity because it might well have rung a few distant bells in his subconscious.

His own paper had been scheduled on the first day, which was nice because it got the thing over and done with. He had presented it to the directors and administrators group, a fairly select body that had met in one of the smaller meeting halls of the conference centre. This he found much to his liking, as he hated addressing large crowds. They had a confusing effect on his speech, as if the god Mercury had unloosed his power on language. He would say things that made perfect sense to him in his measured, presentation voice, only to have his audience stare in mystification, whisper to each other behind their hands, or break into laughter. The words he thought he had used were not the ones that came out of his mouth.

On one memorable and mortifying occasion, in a paper on American cultural imperialism, he had referred to Manifest Destiny as 'manifold density' throughout the entire 20 minutes.

This presentation, he felt, had gone really well. The projector had behaved, his slides had been compatible with the system used in the lecture room, he had followed his text and cues perfectly, and had ended on time. The mark of his success had been the effusive congratulations of Dr Horn-Parforce, the session chairman, and the absence of a single question from any of his colleagues.

Doris worked at her desk in the room they called the office in Amanita Crescent. When they had first moved in here they had called it the nursery, but by now they were out of the habit of it. For some years it had been fairly clear that there wouldn't be any beautiful little blonde goddesses with names like Galatea or Thetis or Arethusa. That's how life was.

The house was curiously quiet this evening. With Bill away there were none of the small noises that one heard, even with a silent and preoccupied partner. No rustle of newspaper or shift of body in a chair, no clink of coffee cup, or clearing of throat. Often in the evening he would be listening to his music. Just recently it was Bach cantatas, and before that string quartets. He went through phases.

She had a lot of work to get done. Far from resting on her extensive family money, she had kept a number of projects on the go since their marriage. Her undergraduate degree was in public administration, and she continued to run a small consultancy business. She was writing up an analysis of social programs for the regional council, and not getting anywhere. She was tired of wrestling with intractable figures that the stupid councilmen would probably never read anyway. And if they did, they wouldn't understand them.

Besides, sex and her temporarily single man kept getting in the way.

Bill and Doris slept together, although these days that was all they did. They had experimented with sexual union when they were first married, and had continued for some years before each realized that nothing much was happening.

Poor Doris. Even after the stark realization that the museum director she was assembling couldn't actually do anything for her in the orgasm department, she remained convinced that she might actually experience climax were it not for the ease with which he

91

either failed to put down the book he was reading, or wilted before the critical moment. She had been tempted on many occasions before they gave it up, to thump him unconscious 30 seconds before the cusp, get herself athwart his hawse (as the mariners in her family would say), then get on with it, only waking him afterwards to enquire if his passion, like hers, had hit like a nor'easter out of the Bay of Biscay. But she never did.

Things were so much better when they were away on vacation. Anywhere away from the routine distractions and it was like fireworks. Trouble is, since he became director they hardly went away at all. She often compared her sex life to an Olympic event; it happened once every four years, and each time on a different continent. It was that damned museum! But that was where he belonged, by God, and she would see to it that he stayed and remained a success. Her project would not fail!

But she wished there was something more she could do…

The conference organizers had laid on an exhibition at the city art gallery for the second evening. Or, at least, the *vernissage* of this particular *exposition* had coincided nicely with the conference dates, so they had worked a *soirée* into their schedule. Delegates were invited to show up in the galleries at 6:00 p.m. for drinks and snacks, followed by the mandatory ribbon cutting and speechifying. Anker was here for the food and drink and conversation; he had had just about enough of people giving speeches to other people, and even though he had attended the minimum necessary during the day he was punch drunk with them. It was time to turn the tables; drunk on punch was the way to go. He avoided the bowl labelled 'non-A.'

He began to circle the exhibition gallery, holding a glass filled with an opaque pink fluid in which pieces of fruit were screaming for help. The exhibition halls were impressive; a large, well laid-out modern building with comfortable floors, soft lighting, and a feeling of spaciousness. He wondered idly where their funding came from.

He was not really looking at the works of art, partly because for any museum person it was a bit of a busman's holiday, but also because of the densely elbowing throng chattering away amongst itself.

Phyllis Stein, administrator of a small but equally richly endowed gallery, crossed his path with some deliberation.

'Bi-ill! How nice! Long time no see!'

She placed a ringed hand curvingly on his sleeve in a gesture of intimacy that was quite incongruent with their relationship. They hardly ever encountered each other, except on occasions like this. Her perfume smelled expensive. She swished her fruit. She was a brittle, silly woman with a tinkling little laugh and come-on body language. The punch was obviously doing its work, and the body was coming-on.

'What a lovely show! Did you ever think there was such artistic talent this far west?'

'I haven't had a chance to look around much.'

'Oh, I know! Too many other nice things to look at!'

She squeezed his arm and pressed a little closer. As he looked at her face close to his, closer than he ever saw his own face in a mirror, a sense of appalling desolation washed over him. All the tiny human flaws, normally masked by distance, familiarity and mascara, were revealed. The little nose hairs, the wrinkles filled with powder and wax, the bright fleck of lipstick on one tooth, an incipient mole. Yet, as he was repelled, so he was attracted. A perfectly counterpointed siren song of desire and loathing. He tore his gaze away and scanned the mob wildly for help.

By a merciful chance his eyes locked with those of Stanford Tench, director of a museum of archaeology, a large man in physique and presence.

'Oh, I'm really sorry. Excuse me just a moment please...' and he swung away in a cold sweat.

'I've been meaning to corner you for ages,' began Tench. 'Wanted to run this repatriation thing by you.'

One of the many committees in the Museum of Personkind had been debating the merits of writing the terms of reference for initiating a study into the feasibility of discussing the formation of a committee to examine the problem of whether or not the museum should initiate a repatriation policy. They hadn't got very far.

'We're in the early stages,' replied Anker diplomatically. 'Not really much to report yet.'

'Oh, sure, but you must have ideas, opinions? Eh?'

'Well, the grounds for repatriation are in some sense well established...'

'O, come on! This is just us chickens! Get off your high horse. I mean, look, they didn't want the stuff anyway. The WeWho. Most of it. And if they kept it, what would it be like now? Eh? Probably wouldn't even exist, half of it. The stuff would have got used up and chucked away. Bet on it. So now they want it all back? Come on! Whadda *you* say?'

In view of the public mess that he had left back home, the last thing Anker wanted was to debate the whole subject of returning artifacts to their purported original owners with a liquored-up redneck. Talk about out of the frying pan and into the fire. Some life raft you turned out to be!

'I say that it has to be approached on an individual basis. We can establish guidelines...'

'Guidelines! Bullshit! As an archaeologist I know in my bones— har, har—that what comes out of the ground belongs to whoever digs it up. Makes sense! Wouldn't be there otherwise.'

Anker was stung by this.

'Really? So, how would you like it if a bunch of WeWho broke into a cemetery and started digging up your grandfather?'

'Come on, you can't make your point with wild exaggerations!' countered Tench.

'But it's true! Recent graves have been excavated. This has happened, and you know it has!'

'All right, I'll concede that mistakes get made sometimes. But the point is, almost all of the archaeological material goes too far back for them to have any claim whatsoever. They're migrating peoples; they can't justifiably take ownership of it. Sorry.'

Anker took a deep breath and marshaled his thoughts. I don't know what the hell is in this punch, but it's making my head clear.

'Really? I didn't know we had persuasive data on patterns of migration before the pre-contact era.'

The archaeologist looked blank.

'I'm no expert, but I assume you know where they migrated from and where they're migrating to. And perhaps, also, why they've been where they are now for as long as we have records.'

'He's got you there!' interjected Morton Hampstead, a curator from the east coast who had drifted towards the pair on hearing Anker's comment.

Tench turned to him, colour rising in his cheeks.

Anker seized the opportunity to seek out the booze table again and get a huge refill. No wonder they call this stuff punch! Perhaps it was the release of the tensions of the past weeks, perhaps it was a feisty, devil-may-care side of him that his role as director kept subsumed, but whatever it was he hit the drinks table harder than was customary for him, and his system wasn't really ready for it.

While he was filling up a big, flabby hand flecked with liver spots flopped onto his shoulder. He turned to encounter the ravaged, pendulous face, basset hound eyes, and stooped composure of Lionel Rolling-Stock. He wore a violent flower-patterned vest and sported an overlarge bowtie that looked like an impaled moth. A huge silk handkerchief squirted from his jacket pocket.

Rolling-Stock was an art historian, now retired, who enjoyed himself immensely by showing up at conferences and other heritage gatherings and acting the flamboyant queen, a role for which he had a natural disposition. He was an out-of-date caricature of himself. He knew it, and he laid it on deliberately, intending to irritate and annoy. He was especially annoying to the ordinary gay folk who just wanted to get on with life and mind their own business.

Wafts of tobacco breath intermixed with an alcoholic beverage not available at this table washed over Anker.

'Ah, it's good to see you again, you old bugger!' cried Rolling-Stock in his reedy tenor.

Years ago, when Anker was a young museology student, doing a placement at a prestigious art gallery, he had been approached by Lionel for something more than just friendship. Repelled and upset at first, but not wishing to hurt the old man's feelings, he had rejected the advances as diplomatically as he could. His cautious and not unkind rebuff had proven successful, even though Lionel had written rather graphically to him several times after he had moved to the museum. He wondered at the time if Lionel might not be confusing him with someone else.

There was even a letter in a lavender envelope...

He had wished he wouldn't keep writing, and in the end he'd persuaded him to stop. But they still remained cordial, although he did wish Lionel wouldn't single him out in crowds like this. It was embarrassing and it made him feel... exposed.

'Fucking heroes, that's what we were!'

'Sorry,' answered Anker. 'I must have missed something.'

'Missed something? Ooh! Course you have, sweetheart. Jesus, I wish you went both ways, you sweet boy you!'

'Hey, quiet down! People are looking! Anyway, what's all this about heroism?'

'I was just saying to that fuckhead over there,' he waved a languid

95

paw, 'that I've been out since he was belching up his mother's milk. I am,' and at this point he struck a pose, 'the Ancient of Gays. Listen, when we came out it was an act of pure heroism. Nowadays? Shit, anybody can come out! Politicians, athletes, film stars, artists; it's no big deal to be queer these days. God, it was hard back then, and I'm not just talking about the old carnal machinery, my dear!'

He laughed high and loudly, and heads turned again from a fair radius around them.

It's a great thing, alcohol, thought Anker. Just imagine my reaction to such attention if I was at home and stone cold sober. Great punch, this pink 'A' stuff with its fructal flotsam. He took another long swig.

After a few verbal thrusts and parries, feints and ducks, Rolling-Stock suddenly looked over Anker's shoulder and cooed, 'Ooh, there's that uptight old fart Wesker. I have to go and expose myself to him—metaphorically, of course—just because he hates it so! Please excuse me, my dear boy. It's my role,' he concluded in a hoarse near whisper, and with a ludicrous wink he turned and waltzed over in the direction of a stiff, grey suited gentleman with a long intolerant nose.

Anker caught the high tenor voice crying 'Make way, make way, for the King of Queens...' before he drifted back into the tide of humanity that was washing and swirling around the works of art, a great gabbling, tinkling, shuffling Gulf Stream of drink and empty-headed chatter. He topped up his glass again, leaving out the fruit this time, and soon found himself becalmed in a Sargasso. The crowd circulated, leaving him in an eye of calm. He had come to a halt in front of a wood carving on a plinth. It was a mask made by a carver from a small place in the centre of the island. It was an odd thing. Carved in the middle of the country, but reminiscent of the west. But this guy could carve! His tools must be mighty sharp, and not a hint of sandpaper, unless I'm very much mistaken. Unusual in this part of the country, wood carving—they're noted for beadwork, quill, and very finely tanned deerskin—and a curious amalgam of style, genre and meaning as well... The artist's name was James Indoda Enhle. Bells should have rung there. He felt that this carving must have much more meaning to him than it did, but whatever it was, it slipped away. Too much bloody punch.

After this encounter the evening became a blur. There was some speechifying; the ribbon cutting, and the obligatory praise and con-gratulation passed without impinging themselves much upon his consciousness. He doubtless talked long and wittily with all and sundry, with nary a false step in diction or vocabulary. But he remembered little of this, except at some point in the evening he had found himself in the bar of his hotel with Lionel, laughing fit to burst about something, and not giving a damn who looked his way.

He eventually found himself back in his room in the early hours of the morning, the world precessing in wobbly orbit around him, like the dying throes of a toy gyroscope, and filled with the deep realization that conference attendance was not just a perk at the Museum of Personkind; it was a necessity.

CHAPTER TWELVE

At 1:00 a.m., early on Wednesday, just over a week after the riot and theft of the statuette, Sue Tort backed a big rental truck into place near the loading bay of the museum. The loading bay was let into the east wing of the building at the rear, and occupied a part of the first floor below the display galleries. The lights of the truck were doused and Sue, Terry and their new Carpenter friend settled down to wait.

Insider information is essential to such operations. The activists' informant for this job was none other than the Carpenter who had worked as a restorer before Woodrow Wilson Easel had sacked him. He had got involved in this caper almost by accident. He had been visiting his friend the security guard at the museum the afternoon of the riot—just confirming a few small details and putting a bit of backbone into him—and then he had gone for a coffee across the street, sitting at a table that gave a view of the front doors. He had seen Easel come and go, and he was on his second cup when the demonstrators had shown up.

Sensing the possibility of further mayhem, he had identified Terry O'Weight as one of the ringleaders, and had followed him to his pub. It was a fruitful conversation. Through his friend in Museum Security, he had got the lowdown on the guards' behaviour, and had given O'Weight some very valuable information. Now here he was, having a second taste at sweet revenge. His first taste was the series of thefts he continued to undertake, of course, but this was a separate and potentially equally rewarding issue.

After much nervous waiting and drumming of fingers on the steering wheel, the small rear exit beside the loading bay doors opened and a uniformed object stumbled woozily out.

'Go!' hissed Tort. 'I'll stay with the truck!'

Terry jumped from the passenger door, and staying out of the line of sight, headed for Rourke Mutcer's office window. He had a large cylinder strapped to his back and he carried a respirator.

Tonight, as usual, the guards who should have been patrolling the whole building and checking for things—like intruders, for example—were gathered in the rear loading bay and getting solidly into their first case of a dozen beers. The theft of the gold figurine and the subsequent investigation had, so far, had little or no effect on their established 'routines.' It was simply business as usual in museum security, thanks to the indolence of their chief.

There were four of them; ideally, one for the front door, one for the rear loading bay, and the other two to patrol each floor in turn, sharing the west and east wings between them. That's just great in theory. In practice, four into twelve goes three. Three bottles each, so by 10:30 that night they were all in great shape.

Around this time, according to the Carpenter, the guards would switch off the automatic alarms briefly, open the small rear door, and take it in turns to relieve themselves in great sudsy gushes against the garbage dumpster. It was easier than going back through locked doors to the washrooms at the front of the building. Even as early as November a deep, angled snow bank against the dumpster sported dozens of neatly drilled yellow-rimmed burrows.

Now with the small door ajar and the alarms off, O'Weight went to force Mutcer's office window open with a prybar, only to find it already unlatched. Celebrating his good fortune, he swung inside, and closed the window carefully, making sure that the alarm sensor on the sill was reconnected before the relieved security guards turned the system back on. The ventilation ducts in this part of the building were carried on steel straps attached to the load bearing beams and concealed by a false drop-ceiling in the corridor. It was a matter of a few minutes to climb onto a packing crate against the wall, remove a ceiling tile, and begin emptying the contents of the cylinder into an access hatch in the ductwork.

A short way down the corridor the last of the guards was tucking himself in and switching the alarms back on. As they sat around in their booth, owlishly contemplating the empty case of 12, and wondering if they should start the next one, the nitrous oxide in the ducting began to have its effect. Their heads began to roll slowly around in wobbling circles, like the last moments of a humming top, until their unconscious bodies slid heavily to the floor. Two fell off their chairs like sacks of second-hand clothes, one slid down full length under the table, and the fourth went over backwards. Thud, thud, sli–i–ide and whack! like a coconut hurled at a wall.

Terry, now wearing the respirator, entered the security booth, disarmed the alarms and swiped the bunch of master keys from the key box. He pressed the button to run the loading bay doors up, and Tort backed the truck ponderously in. Once the engine was stopped, he lowered the doors again and, closing the door of the booth, ensured that the fumes and guards were contained. He pulled off the respirator and yelled: 'All right everybody! Let's go!'

The Carpenter leapt out of the truck cab, ran round, and raised the rear doors. Five other men emerged.

'You know what to do! Let's get it done in under two hours. Go!' and they all dispersed to their stations.

The museum was effectively divided down its centre. To the left, as the intruders entered the foyer from the rear, were the administrative offices, and the history, folk culture and archaeology displays. To the right were the objects they were looking for. They headed right and began to ascend the stairs. The first floor was ignored; it contained only models and dioramas, dusty and ill kept from long neglect. The fourth floor was lecture theatre, and ballroom, and the fifth had just physical plant. The second and third floors contained all the valuable displayed artifacts of the WeWho people; the entire 98 pieces of the Treaty Bluff collection. This was their target!

Three to a floor, the self-styled native rights activists began undoing screws and hauling glass and plastic covers off display cases. The fittings required the special security screwdriver and, thanks to their carpenter friend's metalworking skill, each team had one. No time was wasted. They started removing artifacts—masks, rattles, whistles, mostly made ostensibly of wood—which they piled one by one at the head of the stairs. Although they worked frantically, they took surprising care to cause no damage to the objects or the display facilities. Sneezing with dust from long unopened displays, they completed their work in well under the two hours Sue Tort had estimated.

Each artifact was wrapped in a furniture blanket and stowed in the truck. O'Weight counted the material as it was carried in, while the Carpenter wrote it all down. All 98 artifacts they believed. But somewhere between the Carpenter's documentation and O'Weight's thick-headedness, one single carved 'wooden' mask was overlooked, and remained in a corner near the loading bay, quite forgotten and abandoned. It was the mask of the cult creature called the Hare.

'Ho lee shit, what a well-oiled friggin' machine!' O'Weight chortled. 'It's awesome! Just awesome!'

'Quick! One er the bastards started to move!' called a conspirator who was peeping into the window of the booth that looked out onto the loading bay. Terry took a deep breath, sneaked into the booth, and quickly replaced the master keys on their hook in the box. He slammed the key box, shut the booth door, and joined the crew who were loading the last of the artifacts into the truck.

'Okay guys, we're loaded up, let's go! Ho lee shit!'

The rear door of the truck slid shut, Sue Tort started the engine, and the rented vehicle and jubilant thieves roared away into the night. It was just before 2:30 in the morning.

Half an hour later, at just after 3:00 a.m., Rourke Mutcer sidled up to the rear door of the museum. He had parked his car in a side street beyond the parking lot and had sneaked along dimly lit walls. He had been prepared to wait until 3:15 when, according to the guard he had threatened the other day, the security staff would switch off the automatic alarm briefly, and troop out to relieve themselves of the night's second case of twelve. At this point he had planned to sneak in through the window of his office, which he had left unlatched, while the alarm was off. Curiously, the loading bay door was wide open, streaming light onto the stained snow.

He sidled closer, keeping to the shadows. There was no steam arising from the snow, so they hadn't come out yet. He waited a while longer before darting quickly into the loading bay. He peeped through the window into the booth. Bottles were scattered about on the table and the floor, and the four guards were crawling around in blind, whimpering circles like Morlocks exposed to the sun. He opened the door to the booth and looked in. Although completely inured to his own aroma, Mutcer was not insensitive to that of others. Everything that could have happened in a gastro-enteric way to the guards had happened. It hit him like a blast from the charnel pit of hell. Must have been one hell of a powerful brew! He picked up a bottle that had rolled to the door. Funny; looked like ordinary pale ale.

He was mystified as to how they had got into this condition, fortuitous though it was, but he was hardly keen on investigating further. He held his breath, stepped in, grabbed the master keys off their hook in the box and left quickly, shutting the door. Well, this was most convenient, even though he had wasted his time threatening the other security guy. Still, nothing lost. Unthinkingly, he pressed the button to lower the loading bay door, and passed through a smaller interior door that led to the corridor.

He turned right and sprinted down the corridor to his office. The timing of this piece was critical. He picked up his office phone and called Anker's home number. Anker had come back from the museum conference that afternoon. The phone rang and rang. Come on, come on, answer you baldheaded jerk! Willing him to answer he tried to imagine his prey half asleep, jetlagged, fumbling blindly for the receiver. Finally the phone rasped and mumbled. Forcing his voice not to betray relief, and putting on his best security guard accent, he said:

'Misser Anker? Misser Anker? Yeah, this is museum security. We gotta suspicious intruder here you orter check out. Thief. Yeah, inner front door. Okay?'

He waited until heard Anker reply that he was on his way, then hung up.

Next Pork trotted up the stairs (the elevator was still busted) to the fifth-floor mechanical room. Now, where the hell was it? Remember the blueprint. Right! Two large red handwheels with painted legends attached to the wall behind. He seized the wheel labelled 'sprinkler supply: lingerie, menswear, notions, kitchen east'—a relic of the long-gone department store days—and wound it fully clockwise, shutting off the water. The other wheel, which supplied the fire sprinklers in the west side of the building, he left on. It was not his intention to deprive the entire building of fire protection, just the side with the fake Treaty Bluff collection. Even in his madness he felt some compunction to protect some of the cultural heritage. He had completely forgotten the security staff.

Back down the stairs he ran with frequent glances at his watch. In the cleaner's storeroom on the first floor he grabbed a large brown bottle of acetone and a bin of rags. These he carried across the foyer to the first-floor display area. He put the bottle down and dumped the rags out against the plywood side of a diorama.

Mutcer made his way quickly to the front door to ensure that his victim would arrive before the next phase of activity. He unlocked the great oak doors and waited in the glass booth in the foyer, peeping out of the little hatch in the doors occasionally, until he spied a shifting spot of reflected light approaching the museum. As soon as he had positively identified his victim, he picked up the phone in the security booth and dialed the 911 emergency number.

'Police! Thieves in the museum! Fire! At the front door! Quick!' and hung up.

With Anker actually shoving open the front doors of the building,

Mutcer darted back to the doomed diorama, glugged copious quantities of acetone onto the pile of rags, struck a match and ran like hell for the rear of the building. He passed through his office, stepped through the window, and was away across the parking lot. He still had the master keys in his pocket. Even though he was out of the building and in his car in under a minute, the blaze was beginning to show as a satisfying glow in a few windows. He drove home by a circuitous route, not because he thought he was being followed, but simply because he thought it was in character.

The phone rang loudly in the Anker homestead. Nobody ever phoned the residents of Amanita Crescent at 3:15 in the morning. They were regular folk with fixed patterns to match their immaculate lawns. A phone ringing in a house was unheard of at this hour of the morning. People in this neighbourhood even had their accidents or died at more civilized hours of the day. The phone didn't appreciate such niceties; it continued its ringing.

Bill Anker came up from the depths with the sound of the phone weaving itself into his dreams. It rang a number of times before he realized he should do something about it. He was only just back from his conference and still had residual booze, late nights, airline food, and a couple of hours of jetlag to get over. He fumbled wildly at the bedside table, knocking over a glass with a thump, gurgle and clatter.

'Jesus Christ!' croaked a voice beside him. 'That's my bloody bridge!'

Apologizing sleepily to Doris, he found the phone and stuck it somewhere near his ear. 'Wha'?'

'Misser Anker? Misser Anker? Yeah, this is museum security. We gotta suspicious intruder here you orter check out. Thief. Yeah, inner front door. Okay?' and he was awake and sweating.

'Yes, yes,' he replied. He paused, then nodded. 'Yes! I'll come immediately!'

He swung his legs over the side of the bed, stood up, and trod heavily on a partial upper denture; a modern-day White Fang, result of a childhood accident with a swinging spinnaker boom. He screamed and leapt into the air, clutching at his foot.

'Now you've got blood all over it, you clown!' roared Doris, fully awake. 'Good God, look at the time! What the hell's going on?'

'Want me at the museum,' answered Anker, half in his pants, hopping on one foot and wincing in pain from the other. 'Suspicious intruder... 'S what they said. Could be the thief... Stuff missing...'

Mutcer might have changed his plans if he had thought he might awaken Doris as well as his victim. But he had little experience in this area; no one of any of the sexes had ever invited itself between his reeking sheets. Doris Ironside-Anker fully awakened and aroused, did not figure in his plans. Waking the wife along with the director proved to be a key mistake.

So Anker left his wife, fully awake, peeved in the extreme, and mighty suspicious. He rushed out to his car and sped off in the direction of the museum. Not much more than 10 minutes later he pulled into the rear parking lot and hurried around the side of the building to the front door.

The door was unlocked! He stepped gingerly into the dim, echoing foyer, his head sending flashes of semaphore over the silent space. Now, with the nighttime roar of the city cut off by the heavy doors, the place was eerily still. There was no security guard in the booth, no sign of activity anywhere. He stood, uncertain what to do. The stillness and abnormal quiet began to frighten him.

Presently, a sound made its way to his ears; a crackling, popping sound. He thought briefly of the H.P. Lovecraft museum monsters of gothic fiction that might make such a frightening sound, before he realized. Fire! He ran towards the sound and was engulfed by the terrible stench of burning. Burning wood. Burning plastic and fabric. Burning!

Reaching a corner into the display galleries of the first floor, he saw a glow and realized that a huge fire was in progress just beyond his line of sight. He then did a very Anker-like thing; he panicked. He was drawn towards the fire in an effort to extinguish it, and he was repelled from it by the need to get help. So he oscillated violently, dithering backwards and forwards and muttering:

'Wha-do-I-do? Wha-do-I-do? Oh, wha-do-I-do?'

The fire asserted itself in a thump and a shower of sparks, which wafted towards him on a hot breeze. This evidence of the spreading blaze damped his oscillation. He rushed off to the front doors as fast as the tooth marks in his foot would let him, quite without thought for where he was going, and ran straight into three policemen...

Fuelled by a highly volatile solvent, and working on dry wood, paper, cardboard, synthetic resins and wax, the fire soon spread. The diorama bubbled and seethed before the wax of the figures exploded into blue flames. The flames leapt across from display to display until the whole lower gallery was an inferno. An updraft of superheated air carried flames up the elevator shaft and the stair wells in the antiquated, inadequate building.

One after another, display cases on the second and third floors surrendered to the flames. Plastic case tops slumped down in bubbling fumes, sheets of glass shattered and fell, allowing the flames access to the empty displays. Ceiling beams cracked in the intense heat, floors gave way and the half of the building where the fire had started became a flame-filled shell. In half an hour all evidence of the displays had been utterly wiped out.

Except in one sheltered corner location at the back of the first floor. There, a beautiful mask of the Hare lay where it had been miscounted and forgotten by the thieves in their last-minute haste, still wrapped in a furniture blanket. A huge piece of asbestos ceiling tile fell over the corner, followed by a sheet of drywall, further protecting it from harm.

Amidst all the debris of the days to come the Hare would be found by forensic investigators, intact and unharmed.

The Hare is a trickster.

The Hare's real name is N'ufnīvah. He is the jester among the people of the lakes and woods. N'ufnīvah is always up to all sorts of naughty tricks, most of them scatological if not obscene. It is his role to throw discord and alarm and uncertainty into the workings of the gods. And those of people.

Many cultures that have the envious gift of being much nearer to the spiritual and the aesthetic than materialistic Westerners have tricksters in their mythologies. The white people from the strange East who now populated this land had thrown away their tricksters, along with the rest of their *real* gods. You have to go back in their mythology for more than a millennium and a half before you find the Celtic Merlin. He was one. Then there was the Norse jester Loki. Even though the West has turned its back on its tricksters, it would do well not to ignore them in other cultures. They have power, even in captivity.

The survival of this particular piece, in the face of almost impossible odds, is near proof that our lives are shaped by greater forces than we apprehend. This mask was Anker's nemesis, and its survival virtually guaranteed trouble. Pork Mutcer would see to that.

N'ufnīvah the trickster, the jester and wag, was at the heart of the guilty secret that gave the smelly head curator such power over his director.

It would have taken ages for the three policemen to extract any information from the hysterical Anker at the best of times, but the smoke and sparks told them all they needed to know. They rushed him outside, sat him in a police car, and confirmed the general alarm.

Almost before their call was made, fire trucks screeched to a halt in front of the museum and thundered into the rear parking lot. It was the second time in just over a week, but this time hoses were unreeled, and men ran to stations as sirens, alarms, bells, and the roar of the fire filled the air. Had the fire department been right on the spot at the outset of the blaze, they could have done nothing. At this stage they sought merely to contain the inferno and prevent its spread to the other half of the museum and the adjacent buildings.

Anker watched all this with a numb horror. It is typical of the man that he had no inkling of the fact that the inferno he saw was the Phoenix of his new museum. From these ruins his dreams would arise. But he existed without any coherent thought, in the immediate present. Neither did he hold any realization of the incriminating position in which he had been found. He only knew his beloved museum was burning down and that he had to get away; get the sight out of his eyes, the smell from his nose, and the awful sound from his ears.

Suddenly, all the hysteria, the twittering and dithering, resolved itself into a purpose. A stupid, pointless and extravagant purpose, but action nevertheless. He suddenly burst from the police car and ran in great limping, loping strides to the rear car park, the flames casting dazzling, ruby reflections from his sweat polished dome. Foolishly, the police had left him alone and had become quite busy elsewhere. His escape would eventually be regarded in the worst light.

In the rear security booth the smell of smoke through the ubiquitous ducting caused the boozed, doped and stinking guards further anguish. The master keys had disappeared from the key box and all the doors were locked. Electrical power within the building had failed so the loading bay doors would no longer respond to the button. They rushed around the loading bay and the near corridors while the heat rose and smoke blinded and choked them. None too steady on their feet anyway, they smashed and blundered into each other in panic. Mutcer had completely forgotten them; causing injury or death would have horrified and terrified him.

Finally, with a yell of joy one of the guards found an electric forklift truck parked in the adjacent corridor. He leapt aboard and fumbled with the controls. His three colleagues, seeing him approach through the smoke, judged their moment and jumped nimbly on as he trundled past at a full five miles per hour. He steered for the loading bay door and stamped the accelerator down. The unaccustomed surge of current fused the truck's contact breakers full on and 200 amps of power surged into the motor. The truck leapt forward, whining like a jet turbine, and gaining a huge momentum from its cast iron counterweight, full load of lead-acid batteries, and crew of four, battered the sheet metal door down and out in one enormous charge.

With a huge whoof of smoke like the opening of a giant pizza oven, the liberated forklift shot out of the aperture with its cargo of stinking, jubilant passengers aboard, and tore around the parking lot, striking sparks from parked cars, fire trucks, and railings, bouncing over hoses, and sending up huge cascades of water. By now the brimstone smell, the lurid flames, the nitrous oxide, and the booze had convinced the driver he'd died and gone to hell. Looming before him was the ungainly running/limping figure of Bill Anker, silhouetted against the inferno and with dazzling flames reflected off his sweating cranium like a mane of fire.

'Arrrgh! Lucifer!' he screamed. 'It's the devil hisself!' and assumed a ramming course.

Anker owed his life to the one well-proportioned guard clinging to the forks, who took the full impact of the collision in his belly. Air whooshed out of two pairs of lungs and great sheets of frothing, half-digested beer drenched Anker. He rolled incontinently off the still speeding forklift and lay face downward in a puddle, bubbling gently, his interrupted sleep resumed.

CHAPTER THIRTEEN

O n Wednesday morning, office workers arriving for the day were appalled to see the burnt-out shell of the museum galleries, still wreathed in smoke and steam. Water was being pumped onto the wreckage, streets were closed for a block round the building, and traffic was diverted. Helicopters from television and radio whomped overhead. The interior of the east side of the building, where the fire had originated (on the left as one faced the front) had fallen in. A heap of black, twisted beams and charred woodwork, visible through the empty holes of the first floor windows, was all that remained of the floors and the roof. Now that ancient elevator would never get fixed. The central foyer had, indeed, served as a firebreak, so the west side of the building with the history, folk culture, and archaeology displays, and the administration offices on the upper floors, had survived. Water and smoke damage were particularly bad in the gift shop and cafeteria on the first floor, and the basements below were flooded. Even so, that side of the building could be said to have survived intact.

The effort was now concentrated on damping down the still smoking remains and organizing a salvage effort for papers, artifacts, and equipment isolated in the intact western portion. A committee, organized by Mrs Straw and the Board of Trustees in the absence of the director, was investigating temporary accommodations for the administrative files and curatorial records, which were at this moment being hauled out of the upper floors by a crane before they could sustain further damage. Boxes of filthy and meaningless paperwork littered the sidewalk.

Naturally, the administration considered the paperwork far more important than the artifacts, and it wasn't until the conservators arrived that any thought was given to the displays. By great good fortune most of the objects in the history, folk culture, and archaeology floors in the intact side of the building had been protected from both smoke and water by their display cases. So, once the conservation staff arrived on the scene the artifacts were transported to rapidly prepared spaces in the other buildings.

Needless to say, the museum had no emergency plan in place, but there was, however, an emergency and disaster response plan committee—the EDREP—which had met monthly for many years, had discussed disaster plans, and had examined and analyzed the work of other, more organized institutions. The output of this committee, comprising some 13 solid reports in multiple copies, had not yet led to the formulation of an actual plan. The working drafts—along with numerous memoranda, supporting documentation, and books and pamphlets—were among the paperwork being hauled to safety by the crane operator. Fortunately for the EDREP members, the documents would be found to be completely legible, so the members would be able to resume almost where they left off. Several committee members gathered in the street below were already framing the fourteenth report in their minds, although there would be a lot of research and discussion necessary before it could be tabled even in draft form.

The Women's Association for the Friends of the Museum was in its element. Fully half of the WAFM members were delighted, deep inside, for this fabulous break from routine. Ladies who loved organizing were organizing ladies who hated being organized. Tea and coffee and doughnuts were consumed in gallons and hundreds respectively.

The women who served the refreshments were of a particular kind. They were of a generation whose destinies were tied by bonds of matrimony to bulgy boardroom and good-life denizens, reeking of cigars, maleness and importance, about whom a bounded but infinite domestic universe revolved. Condemned for eternity to hover at the edge of brittle conversations in endless and unchanging soirées, they lusted like confined prisoners for the light of stimulating events. They were the ultimate volunteers.

Ah, terrorists could burn down as many museums as they wished, if the collateral release was always as good as this! More tea? The firemen and police had never been to such an accommodating feast. It was like a wake.

A small knot of administrative staff—those employed in this building—stood at the far side of the rear parking lot, chatting in awed voices and wondering if the employee pay-and-benefits files had been rescued. Among them, Sunil Prakeesh was thanking God that his office and all its beloved clutter had been spared, but he was in two minds about the museum's server; that electronic box at the centre of the computer systems. It had probably survived unscathed. This was a relief, in that the databases would still be operable, but wouldn't it be wonderful to revisit the whole system and make all sorts of changes? As it stood, the system was far too simple—simplistic even—and there was so much more that could be added to it! Ah well, it was just unfortunate for the staff that they would not reap the full benefits of the expertise he could bring to them.

Chief of Museum Security Lucian Limace eyed the ruins in something near incomprehension. Too much had happened in the last week or so; years of tranquility and ease had been torn from him, and his control—what there was or had ever been—was spinning away. And his signature on that report, still inky wet in his mind's eye, was giving him the creeps.

Others who worked in the remaining four buildings filtered into the vicinity, having taken time off to survey the disaster.

Woodrow Wilson Easel contemplated the mess as he organized his staff in the chore of removing objects from smoked glass cases, swaddling them in plastic bubble wrap. So all the copies had gone! Burnt up like they had never been. Mutcer had done his job in spades! But it was so long since he had set a fire himself, that he was deeply jealous. Dangerous game he played as a kid; disused barns, abandoned houses, once a new car. So, how many people knew they were only copies? He ran an inventory in his mind; his staff and the reproductions people, of course, but how many others? Anker; he knows. Curatorial people? Only Mutcer. Everybody else thinks the real ones are lost, and them that know the truth are too shit scared to admit it! If I can't make something out of this whole mess and come out ahead, then I ain't the man I know I am!

Rourke Mutcer was making a show of selfless devotion to the museum by pitching in to the dirtiest jobs, moving soggy boxes of smoky papers and helping to shift charred furniture. While he worked he was contemplating last night's performance and congratulating himself on the thoroughness of his plans. His first floor office was a ruined mess, but he could hardly care. He had moved out all the important files over several evenings—like Easel, he kept files on people, although he was rather inept and nowhere near as systematic—and the rest of the stuff was pretty well disposable. In fact, it all lent credibility; he would hardly set fire to his own office, now would he?

Everything was falling into place perfectly. Even Baldy had disappeared, sure sign of guilt. Maybe he was in custody already? If not, he would surface eventually, or they would haul him in. Either way, the whole scheme had worked so well they might throw him out of his job before he could be forced to resign. He, Mutcer, might not need to apply any further pressure!

As salvage work progressed, housing of displaced staff began to be considered. Building Two, an ex-bus garage, was just across the rear parking lot from the main museum, and thus easily accessible. It had a great deal of open space down its centre and was used for storing some of the larger artifacts, such as ploughs, steam engines, canoes and furnishings, and also many smaller items that would never be displayed. There were also smaller rooms with lower ceilings adjacent to the high bus barn itself. They had originally been offices and workshops for the transport company technicians. The glass and steel roof spanning the central open space leaked incessantly and pigeons nested among its rusted beams. All the objects had to be covered with tarpaulins or polyethylene sheets, which were liberally daubed with guano. The huge main doors opened onto the parking lot, but the bus garage stood on a slight slope, so that its rear exit went down a flight of stairs to the street.

This was the best place, though hardly ideal, for temporary housing, so desks, filing cabinets, computers and other administrative necessities were soon loaded onto dollies and moved over. The artifacts took second place and perforce trickled over to their new home over a period of days.

CHAPTER FOURTEEN

W elcome to the land of the living,' boomed the familiar voice. 'If I didn't keep an eye on you 25 hours a day, I don't know what the hell might happen.'

Bill Anker opened his eyes slowly. He was lying in his own bed in Amanita Crescent, morning sun was streaming in, and he was between clean sheets. He'd just had a horrible nightmare. The museum had burned down, and... Oh, no! It was *true!*

'All right, all right! Lie down. Take it easy.' Doris shoved him down firmly with a hand on the chest.

He ached all over. He was bruised in several places, his heel ached, and he had cuts and grazes on his shins, which Doris had dressed while he was unconscious. It was a miracle he wasn't much more badly injured. He could remember the fire, meeting the police, running to the parking lot, but after that... nothing. Doris had no idea how he came to be lying unconscious in a puddle and stinking like a brewery. It was utterly beyond her comprehension.

She had grown increasingly uncomfortable and suspicious after he had left, knowing that if there was shit to be stepped in, his shoes would surely find it. Finally, she had phoned the museum and had been unable to get through. Alarmed, she had jumped into her car and hurried off to the scene.

Sure enough, where Bill Anker was, so was trouble, although the blazing museum was a bit hard to take. He was lucky she found him. It was more by accident than anything else. Backing her car round to park in a narrow space, she had caught the gleam of his cranium in her headlights. She checked that he was still alive, bundled him into the car, and took off. Now she had him back at home, out of harm's way, and looking vulnerable and damaged in his pyjamas.

'What...? What happ...? When did...? Wha...?'

'Shut up and drink this.' She shoved hot black coffee at him, assuming incorrectly that he had been plied with booze, temperate though he usually was.

'How did... I... How did I get home?'

'I retrieved you. Getting to be a habit, isn't it?'

'I don't know what happened. The museum on fire! Oh, my God, what am I going to do? What *am* I going to do?'

The memories all came flooding horribly upon him.

'Do? Realize your dream, that's all! You'll have to have your new museum now, won't you? Sure, a lot of artifacts have been lost, and that's tragic, but there's more in storage.'

Little did she know exactly how much more there was in storage.

'It's a new start, for God's sake! Why in hell aren't you delighted?'

'There was no security guard there!' he mumbled. 'The fire! And I was running... And the police grabbed me...'

'Police? Stop right there!' she commanded. 'What's this about police grabbing? Start at the beginning and go logically and concisely to the end. Do *not* leave anything out.'

So, he took another gulp of coffee and told her the whole story as far as he understood it. How the doors were unlocked, how there was no security guard in the booth, how he had discovered the fire. Finally, he told her of the three policemen he had met while leaving the building. That explained the phone call she had had earlier, asking his whereabouts. She had told them to mind their own business. Trouble is, it now appeared that it was their business.

'Okay Bill,' she said, when he had finished. 'This whole thing is very damned fishy.'

'I know. Why was the door unlocked? How did the fire start? Security phoned me, but they weren't there when I arrived...'

'Yes, the whole thing smells. Fact is, somebody is trying to frame you. You were set up to be right there at just the right time.'

'And the police...'

'Exactly! And you, my sweet, are the prime suspect. You have the motive, you have the means, and by Old Nick's ebony pecker you were caught red-handed!' (He wished, sometimes, that she were not quite so coarse, but at least she kept it for their more intimate moments.) 'And the worst thing you could be doing is skulking around here. You should be at the museum, or the remains of it, bold as brass.'

He panicked again. 'No, no! I can't! I feel terrible. I'd never be able pull it off...'

His protestations were ignored. She was right, damn her. If he wished to commit professional suicide, hiding in bed would do it. But he couldn't go to the museum, he just couldn't. Admit it, he said to himself, you're a lousy Viking. You're just not assertive enough. You really should take that course through Human Resources. He would apply next Monday if she would just let him off the hook. No, he couldn't face the thought of meeting people and looking them in the face. The thought horrified him. He'd much prefer to just stay in bed and sulk.

The Ironside in Doris came to the fore.

'You will go to the museum, by God, and you will make exactly the impression you ought to make, and have to make. I will see to it!'

Eyes don't blaze, no matter what the novelists say, but hers did.

She hauled him out of bed, got him dressed and respectable and then said, 'Now stick this in your ear and shove this in your pocket.'

'What is it? I'm not deaf. A radio?'

'Yes. A simple transceiver. Now, put this in your buttonhole. It's the mike. No, no, no, it can't be visible! There, behind the lapel.'

She stood back and appraised him while he squirmed.

'You'll do. It's a good set. I got it from that electronics shop for your bloody little nephew Stevie's birthday, but the little jerk'll have to make do with something else. I have grander schemes!'

'No, Doris, no! I will *not* be radio-controlled!'

He was almost in tears. Damn it, she kept close enough strings on him as it was, without having her voice in his ear every waking moment. This would be intolerable. He prepared to dig in his toes.

'Do you like your job?' she forestalled him sweetly.

'Well, actually, at the moment, no.'

'Oh, yes you do,' she caroled. 'You love it. And you're keeping it. I haven't greased up everybody I know in this town for the last 10 years to get you where you are for nothing.'

He was stung. 'Oh, come on! That's not fair! What about my professional qualifications...'

'Qualifications, horse balls! You don't have the qualifications to clean finger marks off washroom walls.'

'But degrees in the social sciences...'

'There are no social *sciences*. You have an *arts* degree,' she replied, dismissing it as if it had come off the back of a matchbox. 'Now listen. From now on, *dearest*, and while this crisis lasts, you and I are going to be in direct communication. I am your controller. I will be able to hear your conversation and dictate replies to you in the earphone. It fits right in your ear. Should anybody notice, you may tell them your hearing is temporarily damaged.'

Little did she know, it would be by the time this caper was over.

'Now, I will drive you to work and wait in the car while you do your stuff.'

114

She really did love him. Looking at her harshness, the way she pushed him all the time to be better than he was, the way she pulled the social strings behind his back, and the innumerable other little things she did, one could be a mite critical. But that's the surface. Deeper down, in places he did not find very often, and where even *she* seldom went, there was an enormous capacity to love and cherish. The naval Ironsides had suppressed this weakness in all their offspring, but as soon tell an ambitious acorn it isn't going to become the keel of a mighty warship.

Doris drove them to the museum and parked.

'Now listen. As soon as anybody looks like coming up to speak to you, or you approach anybody, tell me their name in an undertone. Try to act normally. No, correction; if you act normally, things will get worse! But say what I tell you! Our success relies on your faithfulness. Got it?'

She watched his reluctant passage across the parking lot with some concern, and saw him join the group of employees on the periphery of the safe area behind the yellow tape. As he arrived among them, he was spotted by a journalist, who hurried over.

'Mr Anker, can you give us any information on this terrible disaster?' or some such trite opener.

'Well, yes, I can. You see...' He suddenly jumped as if he had been stung, his face twisted in agony, while a tinny, demented noise emanated from the vicinity of his left ear. This was tinnitus with a vengeance. 'Ahh... I mean, no. No comment.'

'Listen,' said the tiny gnat voice. 'In future, no comment to all journalists and other scum of the same kind. We save defence for where it'll be most useful. Carry on. Over.'

Now he had been spotted in the crowd he was soon surrounded by members of the Board of Trustees and other higher museum employees. He was able to remain sympathetic and noncommittal with only a few painful aural goads. As he turned from discussing salvage operations with a tearful but stoic Mrs Straw, he saw his ultimate challenge heading for him. It was the chief of police who he had met all too personally a week previously.

'Ah, Mr Anker, it's delightful to make your acquaintance again, albeit in such dolorous circumstances. We are very anxious to speak with you. Is there somewhere private we could go?'

'Yes...' He winced. 'I mean, no. No, there isn't.' He paused with head on one side, as if listening. 'If there is anything you wish to discuss with me...' he resumed mechanically, 'we can discuss it right here.'

'What I wish to discuss is a rather personal and painful matter which I think you will find extremely embarrassing if aired in public.'

'All right, I'll... Ow, Christ!' The tinny, buzzing voice reached a crescendo and then subsided as a little colour came back into his face.

'I'm sorry, I have a little trouble with my ear.' With an effort he continued, 'I am not accustomed to having police officers... Dropping rather unsubtle innuendos... In front of my staff and my Board of Trustees... If you have any charge to make... I would suggest that you follow formal procedures.'

The chief stared steadily at him for at least 15 seconds. 'Once we have completed interviews and done a full forensic investigation, we'll need statements from everybody. You in particular. Please try to keep yourself available, won't you?'

And he turned on his heel. He had plenty of others to interview today, and time was pressing.

The people around Anker were mystified, not the least by the new assertive director they had just seen in action. Chief of Conservation Easel, who had overheard the exchange with the police chief, was thinking fast. It looked like Mutcer had done exactly as told, even as far as putting Anker in the shit. Looks like a bee-oo-tiful frame-up to me. Good dog! Let's go turn the screws on Anker just a little bit.

He sashayed up to Anker and looked from side to side to ensure they would not be overheard. The director treated him delicately whenever possible. He knew his power, and shrank from curbing or limiting his influence on almost every aspect of the museum's functioning. If Easel ran the museum that was okay with Anker as long as things remained cordial. Some things are better left on intellectual and emotional backburners.

'All gone. Know what I mean, eh? Lucky we're a farsighted bunch in Conservation and Reproductions, eh? But I wanchew to know, that whatever happens, I'm behind you one hunnerd and ten percent. The whole way.'

Anker nodded and smiled weakly, ignoring the patent insincerity. The best kind of friend to hold on to is the one who could so easily become your enemy.

Doris was having none of this. She loathed the man and had smelt his manipulation and treachery for years. In retrospect perhaps she should have left it alone, but her new-found power was proving hard to curb. Easel was a few paces away with his back to Anker when she began dictating.

'I would just like you to know...' said Anker in a loud voice, and then in an undertone, 'Jesus, Doris, have you gone mad?!' Then loudly again as Easel turned back, 'that I am not in the slightest taken in... By your unctuous and insincere concern... Please be assured... That I can handle this... Perfectly well by myself.'

Now he/she had really blown it! Anker was dumbfounded and scared. Easel said nothing, but stared daggers for half a minute before turning for the second time and walking away.

'That was horrible! Horrible!' muttered Anker under his breath. 'You shouldn't have made me do that. He's dangerous! I don't want to do this. I want to go back to bed. Oh, no! Here comes Mutcer.'

Here indeed came the next challenge; old Pork, dirty with ashes and damp from soaked property, but still aromatic on his own account. Anker saw that he was quite obviously attempting to impress all with his selfless devotion, above-and-beyond-the-call, blah, blah, blah. Quite the caring, selfless, altruistic role model. Creep!

As he approached Anker, Mutcer looked around to make sure they would not be overheard.

'What a terrible, terrible business Bill! What a disaster! It was an awful shock to hear about it on the radio this morning. Is that when you heard?'

'No, last... Oof!... yes, on the radio this morning.'

'Hmm. Funny how this should happen so soon after I brought the matter to your attention. Hell of a coincidence, eh? Sort of information would be dangerous in the wrong hands, wouldn't it? Especially on account of you-know-what. Police asking awkward questions, are they? And I've got so much evidence that would be interesting to them, haven't I? I'm sure you understand.'

Bill said nothing as Doris bit her tongue at the microphone. Enough overreaction for one day.

'Anyhow,' concluded Mutcer cheerily, 'you stick with it, Bill.' And he elbowed him in the ribs with vulgar familiarity as he turned away. 'Understand?'

Bill Anker understood only too well. He was so tired of being pushed around by every shithead in the museum, so tired of being manipulated and having decisions made over his head. And now he was horribly scared of Easel. And he was horribly scared of what

Mutcer might do. He was tired of being told what to do at home and in the office. He was so sick and tired of trying to be somebody he very obviously wasn't and couldn't be. He wanted to go to bed and sleep forever, he wanted to quit his job, he wanted to staff the damned checkout at the grocery store. Most urgently, he wanted to go home and get completely shitfaced.

Around noon, emotionally exhausted and nearly deaf in one ear, Anker made his apologies to the salvagers and organizers and headed for the car park. Sympathy was on his side. They all thought he was bearing up extremely well under the shock.

Doris drove them home in triumphant silence. She had much to think about. His debriefing would follow their customary late afternoon gin and tonics.

Early that same morning, in the dismal kitchen of a house in the old part of town, the burglary team gloated over the success of their heist.

'Unbelievable timing! Unbelievable!' crowed Sue Tort, truly believing that her luck was finally changing. 'We liberate the stuff just before the whole lot goes up in smoke!'

'Amazing,' agreed Terry O'Weight. 'Somebody up is there right with us all the way. Timing? Kee-rist!'

'And they think the whole lot's been torched. That's the beauty of it. Wait 'til we announce we've got it all safe and sound. We'll be heroes! They won't give a shit about us lifting it! They'll be far too relieved. We can't lose, Terry. We just cannot lose!'

The other conspirators gathered round smiling. They were a mixed lot. Two were quite young, both students of political science, and idealistic enough to believe that there was some defence for breaking the law in a just cause. The other three were older, had no idealism—if they had ever had any—and were in it for the money, which was just a little better than pogey. One of these was a big, craggy fisherman from the east coast, and he knew hunger, and he knew the misery visited on the small guy by big government and big business hand in hand. No more fish, nor fishermen. Not idealism at all, but a deep sense of being on the wrong end of things. The younger ones had developed a devotion to this cause and would cheerily follow orders. They hadn't had so much fun in a long time. The older three were, basically, out of work, pissed off and enjoying shit disturbing.

The truck-full of artifacts was parked outside on the street and locked. One piece had been brought into the house. Tort picked up the beautifully carved and decorated mask of E'man'ekaf. He is the man of the woods, a cult figure of a people who are among the finest artists and wood carvers in the world. Generation after generation they have produced the loveliest, finest and most powerful images in cedar and alder. This one was made of neither of those materials, but Tort didn't suspect that.

E'man'ekaf haunts the forests and calls through his round, open mouth. He gives children nightmares. He would soon give Tort and her lieutenant a real beauty. As Tort looked at the lovely thing, she was suddenly struck with an ugly thought.

'That fire!' she exclaimed, fixing O'Weight with a wide-eyed stare. 'How did it start, Terry? How did it fuckin' start?'

'Nah, nah, wait a minnit! What are you tryin' to say?'

'It's the sort of stupid thing you'd try!'

'No. God. Damned. Way! Out of the fuckin' question! Ask any of these guys. There's no way I'd do a thing like that!'

The others supported him and she subsided, satisfied for the moment, but never sure just how far Terry O'Weight *would* go, given the opportunity. It was just one hell of a coincidence.

O'Weight broke into the brooding silence that followed.

'Do we bring the rest of the stuff in?'

'No, we do not bring the rest of the stuff in,' she replied. Taking a deep breath, she continued, counting on her fingers, 'One, it would take forever up them stairs; two, where the hell would we put it all?; three, the landlord and his drug-dealing brother would probberly see us, along with anybody else who happens by; four, it's safer in the truck, which has a lockable steel door; five, if we have to, we can make a quick getaway; six... Fuck, I ran out of fingers. Well, anyway, do I have to continue?'

'So, we leave the rest of the stuff in the truck?'

'Yes, we leave the rest of the stuff in the truck.'

She took another deep breath.

'Now the next phase,' she announced, putting E'man'ekaf down carefully and turning to face her troops. 'We do not simply announce this to the world and expect the museum to negotiate. We need a middleman, one with more credibility than we have. The best one for the job is the WeWho Arts Council; basically, our client. We're doing this for the people they represent and they'll be grateful enough to mediate for us with the museum. The ground is well prepared!' she concluded triumphantly.

Naivety is so comforting.

Woodrow Wilson Easel was restructuring patterns of allegiance and support. He had gone back to his office in Building Four soon after encountering the new, assertive Bill Anker. It was becoming clear to him that Rourke Mutcer's job of framing Anker was working beautifully. It was also clear that Egg Head had suddenly got all feisty. The last thing he needed was a director who had acquired a mind of his own. The whole thing about Anker was that he was so easy to steer. He took suggestion well and could always be convinced of the common sense of whatever wanted doing. But now he was on the way out by the looks of things, so it was time to discard him. Getting all uppity was he? People don't answer back to W.W. Easel and get away with it! No siree! Time to turn off the charm.

And Mutcer? Well, he'll be nicely in my web, won't he? I got proof he's been playing with the Registry records, and faking reports as well. That's a criminal offence for a start, without the actual fire. And I'll bet I can hang that on him too! Or at least convince him I could. Well, if he's going to be the new director, I better start talking him up. He knows which side his bread's buttered on, and he'll cooperate. New emperor, same old empire. Yes, it's 'be nice to Mr Mutcer week' at the jolly old Museum of Personkind. Ain't it all shits and giggles?

He carefully locked the door of his office—no mistakes from now on—stepped up on a chair, and reached into the cavity above the ceiling tiles for the cardboard file box. He pulled out the folder labeled 'Mutcer' and started adding to the notes there.

CHAPTER FIFTEEN

The chief of police returned to his office after completing his work on site at the burnt-out museum. There was a message waiting for him. Some high functionary in the Ministry of Justice had been asking pointed questions about the stolen Japanese statuette. Diplomatic waves were being made, and they were starting to wash up against his desk. A swift resolution was needed in order to calm foreign relations.

He sat at his desk and gnawed the side of his finger. The view from his office window, high in Police Headquarters, was magnificent. The building overlooked the river and the hills that rose beyond. December had sneaked in this morning, and it was now an unusually crisp afternoon. The pale, almost white, sky outlined the treed hills as sharply as an inked line. A Japanese print of a day. Ironically.

The really beautiful winter weather came in January and February when you have crystal blue skies, loud white snow, and snot-freezing cold. So, such clarity and long-horizon visibility were as welcome as they were unusual. The clarity of the weather did not extend to the case before him. He swiveled his chair away from the window and picked up the three dossiers again from his immaculate desk, but he didn't open any of them. He weighed them in his hand, as if assessing their merit purely on their mass and heft, like an Oxford don with a dissertation.

It fascinated him, this case. That's why he had taken ownership of it. Much of his daily work was administration, so the routine stuff rarely, if ever, got this high. But this one did fascinate him, and he was going to keep it. He had dealt with biker gangs, drive-by shootings, and disagreements in bars that had gone tragically wrong, but this one was different. Things were so often cut and dried; goodies and baddies fell into nice categories. Sure there were frustrations; you knew damned well that the Hell's Angels or the Bandidos were breaking every bloody law in the book, but you still had to respect their rights under the law, God damn them.

But this one on the museum... It was more than frustrating. There was something here that slipped past him like soap in the bath. He always found it helped to bounce ideas off others, so he headed down to the cafeteria, hauling in Sergeant Delios on the way.

'C'mon. Don't know what you're doing, but drop it.'

'Here's the scenario,' he began over cups of cafeteria coffee. 'First dossier: the fire. Arson, unless I'm very much mistaken. A sudden blaze, no evidence of sprinklers working, and a guilty party just walking into our arms. Open and shut, right? See, someone calls in a 911 and our boys show up just in time to catch the director, Anker, in the act of exiting fast. As if to ensure his guilt, he then bolts from their car.'

He sipped his cup, made a horrible face, and added three spoonfuls of sugar. He tried it again. It wasn't any better. He added more milk, but the stuff absorbed it without changing its tarry hue.

'But, the point is,' he continued, 'unless my crook detection faculty is 'way out of whack, this guy is about as guilty as a Mother Teresa.'

'But he was there, he was caught on the spot,' observed Delios. 'And he has the motive: a) he's been planning a new museum for years, and b) they just turned down his proposal. He's desperate. Seen it before. Remember Steerpike?' (The classic case in which they had both been involved, Steerpike vs the State, had ended in an arson conviction.)

'Yes to all of that, but this guy just couldn't do it. Frankly, he just doesn't have the balls. Anyway, have you met his wife? Jesus! He wouldn't cut a fart without her permission. No, he couldn't have done it, no matter how it looks.'

'What about her? Could she have put him up to it?'

'I thought o' that, but she's from a very well connected family. They sit at the right hand of God, y'know. Probably tell him what to have for breakfast. No, too dangerous. Too dangerous by half. And just not her style.'

'So, somebody's framing him?'

'Right on. But who?'

'Well, we interviewed a whole load of them this morning, and quite honestly...'

'Exactly. When did you ever come across a bunch like them? Christ! Start off with Easel: a bloody psychopath, or my ass is the dome of Saint Peter's. He'd pass a psycho test with flying colours! What score would you give him on the P-Scan?'

'The psychopath test? Easel? No, he struck me as quite sincere. Remember when you interviewed him last week after the theft? Psychopath? Surely not!'

'Yup. I saw you nodding, agreeing with him. When you've been around as long as I have you'll learn to spot 'em. They're everywhere, and that's not simply me being paranoid. Just because he's got no criminal record, doesn't mean a thing. Just means he's got better control, that's all. Physical anyway. Probably does high pressure sports to let it all out. He talked you around just fine, but don't feel bad about it. He's damned good.'

'What? You mean his explanation about the theft and being framed?' Delios shook his head slowly, the disbelief on his features writ clear.

'Hold that thought 'til we talk about the thefts,' continued the chief, getting back on track and ignoring his junior's doubt.

'The fire first. I don't know. It seems out of character for Easel. He's the subtle weaver and string puller type, not the out-of-control maniac. These guys sometimes have flings when they're young, but if they're smart—which he is—they put a lid on it. Then there's Mutcer. Lots to gain. But an arsonist? I dunno. Jones? Jones is clean. Pompous ass, but he just sort of smelled right. Same with Prakeesh. As for the rest, I've never come across so many deadbeats and loonies in such a small space. Dress the security guards in white, tile the walls, spray the place with Lysol, and you'd mistake it for any nuthouse in the state. Could be any of them.'

'What about the managers?' asked Delios. 'What did you think of them?'

'Didn't even notice them, if the truth be known. Bland to the point of invisibility. Nah. Person who did this has got to have some human attributes!'

'Mutcer's got the most to gain. Head Curator now, next in line for director if Anker takes a fall.'

'But would he? Would he?'

He thought for a minute while dishes clattered and tableware rattled around them.

'Put yourself in his shoes. Can you see him getting in at night without either setting off the alarms or being seen by security, probably even turning off the sprinkler valve—which is right at the top floor of the building—calling the cops, making sure Anker shows up, and finally setting the fire? It's all so out of character for any of these museum types. It's organization, timing, skill. What I saw of 'em, they couldn't negotiate shoelaces. Mutcer? Is he the dark horse, then?'

'Should we put a watch on him? We can assign a couple of guys.'

'Nah. If he set the fire, he's done his thing. He won't do anything else. I think we're going to have to wait on this one. Forensic's still got a lot of work to do anyway. Patience. See who makes the next move.'

He sat in thought for a while. 'But if it all points to Anker, we might have to pull the little bastard in…'

'Then there's the petty thefts.' Delios broke the silence. 'Dossier number two.'

The chief picked up the dossier. 'Well, mostly petty. But they're pretty bold if they're lifting gold statues. Especially this one, which is now the centre of a diplomatic shit storm.'

'So, you think the statuette was part of the same job? Not an isolated incident? Unrelated?' Delios wanted to assert his initiative by suggesting another investigative track. 'See, the purses and stuff are just quick lift and run things, whereas the statuette was planned. The right screwdriver and so on.'

'Well, it could be, but let's not get too complicated, shall we? How many criminals do we actually want wandering around? It's a museum, not a friggin' biker clubhouse.'

'Inside job then?'

'Yeah, looks like it. And this is where friend Easel enters the picture.'

'That screwdriver…' mused Delios. 'Easel had it with him, and he told us why he was there that day. A call from security about loose screws. It sure looks like a frame-up, but you don't believe him, do you?'

The chief snorted. 'Not another frame-up! Please! Look at it logically. All that stuff about finding the screws on the floor! Did you ever hear such crap? And he even had a phone call from a security guard too! My God, there are more security guards making more bogus phone calls around that place than anyone would give credit for.' He thought for a moment.

'No, our buddy suspects the security guard might have seen him sneaking in—and has probably told us—so, on the spur of the moment he concocts some bullshit story about loose screws and a mystery thief, and then tries to deflect our suspicions away by pinning it on the guard. Talk about transparent!'

'But what does he gain by it? It's dangerous to his career! What if he was caught stealing?'

'It's the enormous sense of power, but also the sense of being right on the edge. The danger is what gives him his charge.'

'So he makes out he's being framed?'

'Yup. And then, to cap it all, he says,' (here the chief's voice fell to a whisper and he looked surreptitiously over his shoulder) ' "They're out to get me, the whole lot of them". Typical paranoia; fits the personality type to a tee. And in the end it's self-fulfilling, of course. Yes, they are out to get you! But I watched you over there on your chair by the door; he had you taken in, no question. But don't let it get to you. As I said, he's good! Very good!'

The chief rubbed his hands in satisfaction.

'Yup. I think he's our boy. But I don't think we can move just yet. We need lots more than just circumstantial...'

He finished his coffee with a shudder right down the spine.

So, for the one time in his entire life Easel had told a story that equated with the unvarnished truth and, just that once, the truth as he told it was greeted with contempt and disbelief.

'One thing we're doing,' reminded Delios, 'is checking the security camera records. Wonder how far they've got?'

'Yeah, okay. God, I'm slipping! Check the technical people on that, will you? Shouldn't have taken 'em a week!' Delios made a note on a napkin. 'Right then. Dossier number three: the riot. Where do we go with this one?'

'Well, the riot wasn't a cover for the theft, if what you say about Easel is true.'

'It sure wasn't. Look at it! The whole damned museum swarming with cops? That would be brilliantly inventive of somebody, wouldn't it? No, no connection. Rule it out. So where do we go with this one?'

'Nowhere,' answered Delios quickly. 'Unless the museum presses charges. It was a legitimate demo that got out of hand, and nobody to point a finger at.'

'Well, you're the bloody cheery one, aren't you? But you're right, God damn it! A few demonstrators booked for disorderly, a couple of hundred bucks in fines at the most, and a big bill to the city for the cleanup.'

'I was reading this stuff in the file about the ringleaders. We've got quite a lot on them.'

'Yes, but notice how they always stayed just this side of the law. A few petty offences for the thick one; O'Weight? And the skinny bitch? Nothing.'

'They're good at what they do, I will say that for them,' admitted Delios grudgingly.

'Yeah, well don't start admiring 'em. They're responsible for enough civil disobedience to put 'em inside for a good spell. In a civilized country people like them would be used for experimental purposes.'

'You're not...!'

'No! Course I'm not! It's this bloody awful coffee talking. Let's get out of this building and find something decent to drink!'

They left headquarters and headed for a corner coffee shop. The sky was as clear as a bell, but dense clouds obscured the three dossiers of the Museum of Personkind.

Around 11:00 that morning, Terry O'Weight and Sue Tort stepped out of the elevator and made their way to the offices of the WeWho Arts Council. O'Weight carried the mask of E'man'ekaf, breeder of nightmares, wrapped in a blanket under his arm. It was surety of their intentions and a glorious proof of their success.

'Wait here,' said Tort outside the door of Indoda Enhle's office, and to the receptionist, 'We have an appointment.'

Tort was shown into the office and Indoda Enhle offered her a chair. She looked around appraisingly, taking her time and not making a move to initiate conversation. She remained standing.

'Yes, what can I do for you?' he asked, not liking in the least this mean, thin looking specimen. He had seen her somewhere before, but couldn't recall where. Although she had appeared on the TV news during the disturbance at the museum, which he had watched, her face didn't click immediately with him.

'We represent your rights, Mr Enhle. We're activists fighting to return the original people's heritage to its rightful owners. You've heard of us, I'm sure. We're working to get your stuff back from these mausoleums.'

Now the penny had dropped. That's who she was! Those damned protesters! Yes, he definitely didn't like this specimen one little bit.

'Lissen,' she continued. 'You won't believe this, but just before the museum burnt down we liberated all the artifacts. They're all safe in a secret hiding place. None got destroyed. Now, if you people truly want to get them back you can help us negotiate with the authorities. We're in a good position. We can't fail!'

'What do you mean?' he asked, stunned and playing for a little time in which to collect his thoughts. 'You have the artifacts?'

'Yep! Liberated 'em from the museum the same night it burned.'

Now he started to seethe and boil beneath his smooth business exterior. The damned nerve! Oh, the bloody damned nerve of it! Stealing *their* stuff and then trying to hawk it back to *us* like some Goddamned fence! And that particular collection! He took a few deep breaths and tried to calm down, lest something herniate or explode.

Sue went to the door and whistled Terry in.

'I'll show you.'

He entered in as stately a manner as his carriage would allow, carrying E'man'ekaf uncovered before him like a ceremonial offering.

Indoda Enhle was horrified as the truth of what she had said was made manifest. His hard-earned restraint began to desert him.

'What do you think you're *doing*, bringing stolen property into this building? *Into my office?* How dare you try to implicate me in your crooked dealings by bringing this thing here!'

He paused for breath and then tried to continue in a more controlled voice.

'Listen! Do you know anything, anything at all, about the history of these pieces? No, of course you don't! How could you?' he shouted, self-control wavering again. 'When you've obviously got the education and intelligence of that wall!'

'Don't you goddamn yell at me!' returned Tort, also losing her cool and sideswiped by his lack of gratitude. 'We're only trying to help you!'

'*Help?* Do you think bringing that worthless stolen property into my office is help? I'll damned well educate you, you ignorant trash!'

Now the restraint of years was threatening to evaporate like beads of spit on the cast iron stove back home. Okay, stop! Stop. Keep calm. Don't lower yourself to the level of this pair of deadbeats. Breathe easy and slow. That's better.

'I don't know how you dare to come in here and assume that the Arts Council will have anything to do with this! We would be implicated in a crime! This is a matter for the police as far as I'm concerned. This. Is. Stolen. Property.'

In making his points he leaned close to the pair of them and rapped E'man'ekaf with his knuckles. Perhaps it had been one of Caliban's off days, but more likely the mask was an intern assignment, because the thing rang like hollow plastic. He seized the mask from O'Weight, flung it on his desk and dug at its underside with a paper knife. Sure enough, below the thin layer of pigment he exposed plastic resin, while long shreds of fiberglass splayed out of the hole he had gouged. Holy shit! Calm now, calm now. What the hell is going on here? Are they faking me, or did this really come from the museum? If it did, why's it a fake?

'A fake! A plastic replica! And you got this out of the museum?'

E'man'ekaf was breeding his nightmares.

'We did!' screamed Tort.' We did! We *did!*'

'So, where's the real one then?'

Tort lunged towards the desk, making to grab the fake plastic E'man'ekaf, but with a swing of his arm Indoda Enhle swiped it away. The mask bounced onto the floor and fetched up against the door-jamb. The activists turned to run for the door, while Indoda Enhle lunged toward them, making an attempt to reach the door first. He wasn't finished with them yet.

An office chair beside the desk tangled itself in his legs, and before he could stop himself, he pitched forward onto it. His feet shot out from under him and he thundered horizontally towards them. He caught them at their knees and they plunged onto him, clinging like survivors to a whitewater raft.

The trio roared through the door, demolishing it in a shower of splinters, Tort deftly scooping up E'man'ekaf on the way. They cannoned into a Xerox, releasing a black cloud of toner and sheaves of loose paper, and fetched up against the coffee maker. Great glass flagons of coffee leaped into the air. Admin assistants and reception-ists screamed and fled. The copier flashed and smoked, the breakers blew, and the office was plunged into twilight.

Almost before the Pyrex coffee pots could come bouncing down, splashing their scalding, bitter contents over the terrified onlookers, O'Weight and Tort had abandoned their whooping and scything human raft and bolted for the fire exit, E'man'ekaf securely under Tort's arm.

Indoda Enhle rose to his feet in as stately a fashion as he could muster amid steaming fragments, soaked paper, a black rain of toner, sparking contacts, and the round eyes and mouths of his executive assistants and administrators, brushed nonchalantly at the sleeve of his jacket, and twitched a few splinters away with the toe of one shoe.

'This goes no further.'

He turned and marched regally back into his office and slammed the splintered remains of his door. He wheeled his chair back behind his desk and sat in thought. After a minute or so he poked his nose briefly out of the door.

'And order some more office chairs. These four-wheeled ones are lethal.'

Back at his desk, and once sure of no intrusions, he flopped back down in his chair, and regained his deep and puzzled thought. If they really stole that mask from the museum, why was it false? If they didn't, why claim they did? And what about that fire? And, of all the collections of our art, the focus has to be on *this* one! But the key thing was, should he poke his nose in, or should he just wait and see what would happen?

Low profile, he decided.

'I need access to Building Four.'

The Carpenter and his security stooge were meeting again, this time in a small park down by the river. It was safer because these meetings were getting pretty frequent. Even with a sheen of ice over the edges of the water, and drifts of snow against the legs of chained-down picnic tables, there were still a few geese waddling and pecking around. They should have shown more sense, packed their bags, and headed south to the warmth.

'Nah, wait a minute! I know that's what you brought me here for, but it's not on,' complained the guard.

'I said we'd talk in a week remember? I need to finish the job. I need to get into Building Four.'

'You told me last time that was it. Just once more you said!'

'Well, I mean it this time.'

'Yes, but... shit! How do I know that?'

'You don't. I'm just telling you, that's all.'

'Look,' he whispered, leaning close, 'you're fuckin' lucky I'm here. Do you know what'd happen to me if I was connected with that fire?'

'The fire's got nothing to do with it. And nobody suspects you anyway.'

'Oh, yes, they do! Mutcer, that's who.'

'What the hell's he got to do with it?'

In an unguarded moment the guard's guard had slipped. His double role, in abetting the thefts and in telling Mutcer how to get into the building at night, with the certain knowledge that his information had resulted in the fire, fueled his fear of reprisals. He was in the agony of being caught in the middle of events beyond his understanding. He backed off.

'He was just hinting that's all.'

This seemed to satisfy the thief. 'All right, but watch him. He's as dangerous as Easel. Anyhow, I want Building Four.'

'I'm scared.'

'If it helps you, I'm not going to pinch anything.'

'Yeah, right! Think I'm stupid?'

A brief, meaningful silence.

'So, what are you going to do then?'

'You know I can't tell you anything,' replied the Carpenter, 'so why not just play along?'

'I dunno. I got to think about this...'

'Well, don't think too long. It's getting urgent. I want to get the job over and done with!'

He slapped his pal gently on the back. 'Come on, one last time.'

'Okay,' he sighed. 'I'll find out what I can about Building Four. Call me tonight, eh?'

Now the guard was thoroughly enmeshed and wondering how he had let his friendship get pushed so hard. Together they tiptoed back to the path through the green goose slime and drifts of snow. Goose shit, the island's chief export. A skein of geese had decided to seek warmer climes. They rose over the water, curving gracefully, forming a Vee all in unison, gaining altitude, and pointing their heads south. Clever buggers.

As chief of Conservation, Woodrow Wilson Easel was a perfect example of *caveat emptor*. When the museum jumped on the conservation bandwagon years ago, replacing its blue-collar craftsman/restorers with something similar but in a while coat with an aura of science, it did the same prestigious thing that others had done; it raided established institutions for high-priced and totally untried talent. Some of these imports adapted superbly. Others did not work out so well.

The museum had advertised in international journals for a chief for the new facility. Easel, having outstayed the welcome of a museum in the American Midwest, where he had gone after graduation, applied for the job. He had a professional *curriculum vitae* writer prepare documents for him (he didn't even know what it was, let alone how to pronounce it) and he obtained a glowing letter of reference from his present employer. Axiom: the more glowing the letter of reference, the more likely it is that somebody is just dying to get rid of somebody. In the museum community of a small island country this can backfire, but internationally it is a standard procedure.

With these scant documents as evidence of his professional competence, and applying to an institution that had not the wherewithal to judge otherwise, he was offered the job. His charm at the interview swayed the Board, and the museum was first struck by him, then stuck with him.

Unlike Stephanie Chang's, Easel's training had been rudimentary and inferior, inculcating patterns of reflex devoid of intellection. His training was referred to as 'old school' by the more advanced practitioners. Thus, Easel, for all his facade of science, really had at his disposal only one or two dozen nostrums with which his patients were dosed regardless of their symptoms.

If a wooden artifact was cracked, an intractable grey dough was automatically forced into it and painted to match. If a paper document were stained it would routinely be bleached to within an inch of its life. If leather artifacts were dry they would be copiously coated with a sticky concoction of oil and wax.

It was fortunate for the artifacts that Easel was weighed down with his far-reaching empire, which required continuous maintenance and monitoring. He could not concern himself with the routine treatment of objects, and so they were either treated by Stephanie Chang—his one true conservator—or passively conserved by non-intervention. In his absorption with networks of power he passed much of his busy work down to his subordinates, who were also prevented from doing more harm than good through intervening where restorers of the old school would fear to tread. Preventive conservation—the new and tautological art of looking after things without actually touching them—found fertile ground in this domain.

Easel did do one artifact treatment when he first arrived at the museum, which was unfortunate for the artifact and, ultimately, for his director. He had been presented with a badly degraded wooden mask of N'ufnīvah, the Hare. The joker. Insect action had made the wood extremely fragile and only vacuum impregnation with a synthetic resin could save it.

It was the treatment dossier of the Hare that Stephanie had reviewed earlier. And her views on synthetic materials suitable for consolidating fragile wood were markedly different from his.

One of the least likely materials for this job is cellulose nitrate, or celluloid. It is heavily modified with volatile plasticizers, it is chemically unstable, its degradation produces acidic and toxic vapours, and it yellows extremely badly.

Most of all, though, it is highly explosive. It is the same material used to make gun cotton and cordite. But because this substance had been used traditionally by two or three generations of 'old school' conservators as one of their small handful of nostrums, Easel considered it perfectly suitable.

A thin wooden object impregnated with cellulose nitrate was a bomb looking for a detonator.

CHAPTER SIXTEEN

D oris was wrestling with the events, trying to achieve order in the systematic way of her naval forebears. She needed the same wily diplomacy that Admiral Sir Mariot Arbuthnot must have employed at the siege of Charleston in 1779. Of course, he was also packing a lot of heat...

'All right,' she said, guzzling gin. 'What's Mutcer got on you? What kind of whammy does he have, and why?'

It was Wednesday just before supper and they were sitting in their living room in Amanita Crescent. The flap on the booze cabinet was folded resolutely down and open for business. A mass of bottles in all kinds of shapes and colours of glass sported themselves below shelves of drinking vessels in equally diverse array. Beside the cabinet wine bottles poked out of their rack like massed cannon run out for an alcoholic broadside of Trafalgaric proportions.

Gin and tonics were their favourite tipple at this time of day; they provided a stimulus to thought and a sense of wellbeing in the stomach department prior to the enjoyment of supper. Bill was not into the wellbeing thing at the moment, being too shaken and stirred, but like his gin he was getting drunk quite quickly.

'So, what kind of whammy does he have?'

'I don't know. I just cannot imagine,' he answered untruthfully. How could he possibly admit to the incriminating fiery incident in his past? That was what Mutcer had been hinting at. It was bad enough that the evil swine was a witness to it. Doris would be furious at his stupidity and would certainly withdraw her support (which might not be such a bad thing, the way he felt). He was tired, his ear hurt, the tooth marks in his sole were sore, and his whole body ached from somersaulting over forklifts.

'I just don't know,' he sighed again putting his nose into his glass and downing more gin.

'Let's get this straight,' she growled as she splashed more gin and minimal tonic. 'The bastard's out to frame you for the museum fire. He wants your job, obviously. Which means he set the fire himself. No! Shut up and listen! Here's how it goes: he gets into the museum at night—Christ knows how, but who cares?—and phones you, imitating a security guard. He must have phoned the cops as well. He then waits 'til you show up, lights the fire and takes off. As you appear, he disappears, and then in come the cops. Good timing, I'll give 'im that!'

'But, Mutcer? Would Mutcer do a thing like that?' he replied, reluctantly rising to the discussion, and showing his first interest today in the continuation of his life into tomorrow. 'I know he's damned unpleasant, but to deliberately set a fire?'

'Oh, sure! He's completely out of his tree. Look at it logically: he's going on about fire precautions a week before the fire...'

'That's right!' interrupted her sweetest. 'Maybe he concocted that report himself!'

'Wouldn't put it past him. It was more literate than Limace could dream of. And, he's threatening you with all sorts of 'evidence' that he claims to have. Christ! What am I saying!? What evidence? *What evidence?*' she demanded, boring her eyes into him.

'Well, paperwork... reports, memos. Files and stuff. All kinds of documents...' he prevaricated, starting to sweat under the inquisition.

'His office, my dear, was consumed by fire last night! If he has his 'evidence' then he must have removed it from his office before the fire! So, is he prescient? Got glass balls, has he? Or is he guilty of arson?'

'My God, you're right! If he has the files on...' he paused and retreated. 'I mean, if he has *any* files, he must have rescued them before the fire.'

'Yes! That's a nice little crack in the creep's armour!' She looked very closely at him, and watched him shrink under her gaze. He took another long pull at his gin and avoided her eyes.

'So,' she continued, enumerating points on her fingers. 'He knows, or hints he knows, that you were at the museum on the night of the fire, and he's hinting at having evidence of something in your past association with him. Something that he refers to as "you-know-what," and which is mysteriously connected with fire.'

He quailed.

'And which,' she concluded heavily, 'you claim to know nothing about.' She stared hard at him again.

He couldn't tell her. He just couldn't! She could read him like the top line on an optometrist's chart. She knew he was dissembling just by looking at him. Then, with a deviousness unusual to him, he decided to release another of the secrets that Pork was privy to, in hopes of sidetracking her. The thought of deceiving her sent tremors through his bowels. Not the guilt of deceit, but the fear of exposure.

'Well, there is one thing which, if it had got out before the fire, would have been very embarrassing.' He rattled his teeth on his gin glass, only half theatrically. 'You see, the Conservation Department... Easel... always fussed so much about conditions in the building. So we... ah... that is, all the Treaty Bluff artifacts were... moved out one by one over a long period. The whole lot on display were copies made in the Reproductions labs... out of plastic and... and... stuff...'

'*What?* So that's what Easel meant when he was talking about the Reproductions Department! There were no originals? *None?!*'

His ploy was working; she was totally sidetracked. But even so his dissembling felt horrible.

'No, they're all stored away in Sausage... I mean Building Four. Quite safe.'

She stood up, gin sloshing, and stared at him in amazement, scarcely believing his reluctance to tell her.

'Perfect! It's perfect!' she caroled. 'Why the hell have you never told me? What an opportunity to set that bastard right where he belongs and put you firmly in the driver's seat! Oh, yes! You, my dear,' she announced grandly, 'are going to hold a full staff meeting at which time this valiant action will be given the attention it so obviously deserves.'

Bill was horrified. Unlike Doris, who was always right, he was unable to weigh the pros and cons of any action, especially one so momentous. Things always got blurred and cobwebby in his mind like in dreams. But he did know that if he admitted the deception of displaying two whole floors of reproductions for nearly a decade, he would be vilified. On the other hand, if he concealed it, it would only postpone the inevitable. Faced with this situation, and without Doris's guidance, he would certainly have played right into Mutcer's hands and have tendered his resignation. As it was, he was stuck between two extremely smelly stools.

'Assholes! Dirty, stinking, fucking assholes! By the Christ, *I'll kill 'em! I'll kill 'em!*' Sue Tort roared and screamed at Terry O'Weight.

It was true! She and their carpenter friend had just finished checking the artifacts in their rental truck. O'Weight had wiggled the pointy tool of his Swiss Army knife into the backs of the first few they grabbed. Every single one they checked was made of plastic. Resin/fiberglass fakes! Frauds! O'Weight and one of the others had been obliged to restrain her by force from running amok, smashing and

135

destroying. It was the only time he had ever held her skinny body. Her rage had been almost uncontrollable. To be so close, for the first time in her life, to a position of real influence! To hold all the cards in her hand and watch them turn to crap. It was too much to bear.

Her rages never lasted long. They were usually replaced by cold, scheming logic. After 10 minutes of frothing, screaming anguish she went horribly quiet and withdrawn, which disturbed O'Weight and his crew much more than the manic raving, which they had seen and heard before. She was ominously silent, smoking cigarettes one after the other in long, bright, blazing drags. She was turning the humiliation full circle and preparing it as a weapon.

'All right,' she sighed at last. 'By the dirty, baldheaded Jesus we'll show these cocksuckers how to play the game! If they had copies in the display galleries, they gotta have the real ones stashed away somewhere. So we gotta find out where, an' how to get at them. We've liberated that crap once; we can liberate it again.'

Double take.

She turned to Terry. 'Get in contact with our inside men. Find out from the Carpenter where they keep this shit, and then get the security lowdown from him. We ain't dead yet, by Christ!'

The booth in *The Puke* was fairly secluded. Terry O'Weight looked around, ensuring that adjacent booths were not occupied. It was early yet, and the place was thinly populated. After ordering a second round of beer, he got down to business.

'Okay, so let's say we want to know about the fac' that all the stuff in the displays turned out to be fake.'

'What about it?' the Carpenter replied cagily.

'You know what about it! You knew all the stuff was fake when we were pinching it, right? What the fuck kinda game are you playin' anyway?'

'I did *not* know it was all fake. I thought it was genuine, same as you.'

This was untrue; during his stint with Easel's department the Carpenter had learned a lot by snooping around. He had a nose for dirty secrets, and he had worked in the same building as the artifact storage where the real ones were kept.

'Why the hell wouldn't it be genuine?'

'I dunno. I don't know nuthin' about museums. Real, fake, what's it to me? Who cares?'

136

'Well, your boss obviously does.'

'She just about fuckin' killed me, and nearly smashed the stuff up as well.'

'Tough shit! I can't help it if you're working for some out-of-control maniac. I'm helping you, don't forget. Christ!'

'Okay, okay! But we now want the real things, not some plastic shit, alright? So where the fuck are they?'

This was like stumbling onto a gold mine, thought the Carpenter. O'Weight wants the real things, and he knows how useful I was last time. The stuff's in Building Four, which is *exactly* where I want to be, but for other reasons. And he looks desperate enough to... ahh... negotiate.

'Wossit worth?'

'You want *paying* now? Come on! Last time you came along for the joyride.'

'Listen. You know I enjoy screwing the museum, 'specially that Easel asshole.'

'What? Who the hell's Easel?' asked O'Weight in surprise. 'He ain't got nothing to do with this.'

The Carpenter was momentarily wrong-footed.

'No, 'course not. Just somebody at the museum. Anyway, that's not the issue. You want me to help, but it could get risky. From here on, it's employment, right? Pay and benefits.'

Another amateur, recognizing a talent that could be translated into money, was turning professional.

'All right, all right. How much?'

He named a figure. O'Weight gulped, swigged down half his beer, retrieved his gum from his cheek, and sat back chewing.

'Too much. Think we're made of money?'

'You want my help, you pay for it. Simple.'

O'Weight's brow became furrowed as figures passed through the sluggish grey matter behind the thick bone. Slowly the numbers formed up in lines and were compared to the inventory of his pocket and the limits set by Tort.

'All right,' he said finally, 'we're buying. Now where's the stuff, and how are we going to get at it?'

'Building Four, corner of Clarence and Main. Just down here. I know where all the stuff's stored, and my friend who gave me the info last time can help get us into the building, and out again. Am I good value for money, or what?'

'Sheesh! Who is this guy?'

'Let's see the colour of your money first.'

O'Weight produced a wad of bills and peeled off a few. The Carpenter counted them, just to make sure, and stowed them away. Then he told O'Weight how to contact his friend in security.

'Call him tonight, get him on side. Then, once he's given you the info we can meet and make arrangements for the next heist.'

'All right! How about another round?'

They drank to pocket money and anarchy respectively. The Carpenter couldn't believe his luck. Access to Building Four, *and* being paid for it!

As soon as he left the pub he phoned his security friend.

'Hi. Just a heads-up. Some guy who wants to get into Building Four's going to call you tonight. Unlike me, he's heeled. So, I thought it might give you a little inducement if a few bills changed hands. Hit him up for some cash, and don't undervalue yourself. Oh, and don't tell him I was already asking about Building Four. That's our little secret, eh?'

It was 7:00 that Wednesday evening. *The Puke* was too exposed at this time of night, so O'Weight chose a further establishment, less known to the museum crowd, to meet the security guard. After they had eaten their doughnuts and taken a swig or two of coffee, they got down to business.

'Thanks for meeting. The Carpenter put me on to you.'

'Yeah, that bastard!' replied the Security Guard. 'He seems to think I'm up for grabs. He sure owes me one! So what do you want?'

'Let's just say we want to get access to Building Four one night.'

What the hell was it with Building Four? Him and the Carpenter both. Crown jewels, or what? It was obviously a two-for-one deal, but he would shut up about the Carpenter and his frigging burglaries. Concentrate on the money.

'Wossit worth?'

Here we go again, thought O'Weight. 'Same as I'm payin' your pal.'

The other coloured a little and looked nervously around. He took a long draft of his coffee.

'Look,' he whispered. 'You're fuckin' lucky I'm here. Last time he helped you pinching stuff the museum burnt down. Do you know what'd happen to me if I was connected with that fire?'

This was *déja vu* all over again. He was beginning to sound like a cracked 78.

'We didn't set no fire. I promise you. C'mon! Coincidence.'

His tongue flung his chewing gum from one side to the other.

The security guard knew they hadn't set the fire; it was probably Mutcer, following on from his threat. But it didn't matter who had done it; either way, he was deeply in the shit.

'Yeah, right! So the cops are going to call it a coincidence as well, is that it? You know my dick's in the vise if anybody makes the connections. This is getting risky.'

'Okay. How much?'

'Three times what you paid him. My pal.'

'*Six hundred bucks?!*' shouted O'Weight.

The pimpled high school dropout behind the counter glanced over at them. Coffee overflowed. O'Weight picked his gum off the table and returned it to his mouth.

'Shut up for Christ's sake! You want everybody to know?'

O'Weight paused, calculating. He took a slow sip and said more quietly, 'Nah, too much.'

'Tough. Take it or leave it. Thanks for the coffee.' And he made to get up.

'Wai' minute, wai' minute.' With the sleeve of his coat caught in a great orange-haired paw, the other perforce sat down again. 'Okay, we'll buy. Let's talk.'

O'Weight and Limace's trusted right hand man exchanged details of security guard shifts, routes and times. O'Weight wrote heavily on a piece of scrap paper with much pencil licking, frowning and what passed for deep thought.

'So? Tomorrow night, eh?'

'Good a time as any,' replied the Security Guard. 'An' I'll supply the packing crate.'

'And this one's shit scared of bones? Stupid place to work. So a scare will do it?'

'Yeah. He'll either run for his life or faint. No sweat. And if he doesn't do either, my friend the Carpenter has a little anaesthetic inducement.'

A wad of money was passed over and hidden quickly in an inner pocket. The Security Guard bought more doughnuts and coffee. He could afford it. Maybe museum security would be a money-making job after all? And in that respect, a great idea was dawning on him.

At night Building Four was staffed by a lone security guard in a small room beside the rear loading bay. He made hourly rounds, circling the building on the hour or the half hour, depending on the schedule of the day.

Late on Thursday afternoon there was some confusion around the loading bay dock when a long, rectangular packing crate was delivered. It was slid to one side of the bay and left for the morning.

At about 10:00 that night, as the lone guard was making his rounds, extinguishing lights and locking doors, the lid of the crate began to rise slowly and horrifyingly. The Carpenter climbed out carefully and quietly, hauled out a backpack and a big canvas bag, and gently replaced the lid. He hoisted the backpack over his shoulder, picked up the bag, and moved somewhat stiffly towards the corridor that crossed the building. According to his friend in the security staff, the guard would have headed down this corridor in an easterly direction some five minutes before. He should now be at the far corner of the storage area.

The intruder made his way silently west along the corridor, in the direction of the Archaeology workshop that was still unlocked. He paused every so often to listen carefully.

He entered the Archaeology shop, dropped his bag on the floor and removed from it a completely articulated human skeleton. He laid the skeleton on a workbench already covered with freshly cleaned bones from a recently excavated burial site. Swiftly, he passed a thin nylon fishing line from a hook on the skull over a light fixture and reeled it out towards a shelving unit. Sliding himself carefully beside the shelves, he drew the fishing line tight and waited.

The guard came clumping slowly down the corridor, keys jingling, and shuffled to the door of the lab. He didn't like the Archaeology shop at the best of times, but in the dark and silence of the night it was horrible. He'd heard stupid stories about the ghosts of disturbed ancestors, but at this time of night them stories didn't seem so stupid... All them bones scared him shitless.

A tiny noise over on the workbench made him stiffen. He shuffled forward, peering into the gloom. Suddenly, the heap of bones on the bench came to fearful life, rattling hideously upwards into a sitting position, arms swinging and loose jaw leering horribly. He screamed once, hoarsely, and slumped down in a faint. Just as predicted.

In minutes the Carpenter had taken the keys from the guard's belt, disarmed the alarm system, flipped the overhead lights on, and opened the loading bay doors. The rented truck with the stolen replicas from the museum still loaded in it reversed in. The doors of the loading bay closed.

'Okay, let's go!' yelled Sue Tort, supervising this one personally like a general, but uncharacteristically in front of the army. 'Guards change shift at one in the morning, so we got plenny of time. Go!'

She turned to the Carpenter.

'How'd it go?'

'Peachy! Didn't have to use the stuff. He just keeled over as soon as he saw the bones.'

'Good. Keep an eye on him. Give him some if he wakes up. Better still, give 'im a little whiff now to keep 'im out. Then drag 'im back to his booth.'

'Right!' He hurried away to take care of this detail.

It was physically easier than the robbery from the museum as no display cases had to be disassembled. Still, locating, identifying and matching all 98 artifacts took a great deal of time. There was an attention to detail here that many common criminals don't possess. But, of course, these people really didn't consider their actions criminal; their cause was just.

This is where the Carpenter came into his own. He knew the systems and approximately where things were kept, and he had the intellectual grasp that O'Weight so obviously lacked. They couldn't do without him, or his friend the Security Guard either. Their money was well spent. All the shelves where the artifacts were stored were draped with dustproof curtains, held in place with Velcro. Many of the artifacts, especially small ones like spoons, whistles and rattles, were enclosed in acid-free boxes.

Even with these complications, the job was done with characteristic speed, efficiency and care. Even so, there was scarcely half an hour left before the change of guards by the time they were finished. Each artifact in the storage had now been replaced with its replica from the rifled museum displays. It was essential that everything be left exactly as found.

'Awesome! The well-oiled friggin' machine does it once again! Ho lee shit!'

For the second time in as many nights, a truck filled with artifacts and jubilant thieves roared out of a loading bay. This time, though, the Carpenter stayed behind to lock up and return to his crate. But unknown to O'Weight and Tort, he had his other little axe to grind first. Helping with the theft was a godsend!

But time was really short. He pulled on a pair of white cotton gloves, quickly unlocked Woodrow Wilson Easel's office, and took a sizeable and heavy bag from his backpack. He climbed onto a chair, pushed a ceiling tile upwards, and deposited some articles in the recess, pushing them far back behind the cardboard file box, so they wouldn't be seen unless somebody was really looking for them. There was a glint of gold.

He put the ceiling tile back carefully, closed and locked all the doors, armed the alarms, switched off the main lights, and returned the guard's keys to the ring on his belt. Almost running through to the lab, he stuffed the skeleton back into its bag, making sure to reel up the nylon fishing line. By the time he was done the guard was just beginning to stir. Finally, he returned to the loading bay and climbed into his crate with his bagged skeleton and empty backpack to await the morning. He'd left his coffee flask and a pack of sandwiches in the crate. Ham and cheese. He sort of wished he had taken a minute for a bathroom break. By morning the wish would become a burning desire.

Everything was exactly as it should have been when the change of shift arrived minutes later at 1:00 a.m., except that a woozy guard was wondering where about three hours of his life had gone. He remembered being in the Archaeology lab and getting a shit scare, and next thing he knew he was back here in the security booth. He felt thoroughly ill and decided he would mention the ghost to no one. He liked his job—apart from them bones—and wouldn't want to lose it. He scarcely believed what he had seen anyway.

Early on Friday morning a truck showed up at the loading bay of Building Four and took away the crate that had been delivered the day before. Just round the corner from the building it stopped, and its driver jumped out, opened the rear, and released the by-now-hydraulically-agonized Carpenter.

Meanwhile, as soon as his shift at the main building was over, the Carpenter's security friend made his way to Lucien Limace's temporary office in Building Two. He had ambitions. He had decided that, given the right circumstances, a job in museum security could be turned into a profitable career. It just depended on what information you possessed, who you knew, and how you applied your well harvested knowledge. He knocked deferentially on the door of the office.

'C'min!' bellowed the familiar voice. The old dugong was propped almost horizontally behind a desk of equal emptiness to the one destroyed and sanitized by the fire. The new quarters already looked squalid, and garbage was beginning to accumulate in drifts in the corners. Although they probably weren't so yet, every surface looked sticky and fetid.

'Whaddayawant?'

'A little word in your shell-like ear hole, boss.'

'Doan fuck with me sonny!'

Limace was feeling surly. The fire, the thefts, and a general sense that events had gone beyond his control were making him more uneasy than he had been for years. He felt as if his masterly ability to do screw-all and get paid for it was deserting him. The Security Guard's timing couldn't have been better.

'How old are you?' asked the Guard, switching tracks and momentarily putting Limace at a disadvantage.

'None o' your goddam business! Jeezers! Now, whaddayawant?'

'Near retirement, I'll bet,' he mused. 'Bet there's almost no financial advantage to staying on here.'

'Nah, look,' growled Limace, almost rising from the prone position. 'I dunno what you're getting at, but y'c'n drop it! Piss off back to your work!'

The Security Guard wasn't fazed. 'A series of break-ins, a mysterious fire, all kinds of shenanigans behind your back, and all preventable by Museum Security. By you, if you were doin' your job.'

'What the hell are suggestin' you little squirt? Geddouda here!'

'I'm not suggesting anythin'. I'm just saying that all sorts of things have been going on around here, and that I know one hell of a lot about it all.'

'Whaddayou know?' asked Limace, a little unsure of himself. The urge to find out what this guy knew began to outweigh the urge to hurl him through the door without opening it.

The Security Guard ticked things off on his fingers, reciting in an almost sing-song voice.

'I know who's boozing all night instead of guarding the museum, I know who's doing the thefts, I know who let them into the buildings, I know who set the fire, and I *think* I know who's been faking fire system reports...'

For the first time in several decades Limace felt that cornered feeling. He clicked his thinking processes into high gear; about the equivalent of second in a five-speed box. If this whipper-snapper wasn't bluffing he could make things fuckin' uncomfortable. Depends how much he knows. But he's a smart little son of a bitch. Always snooping, asking questions. Ah, shit! Maybe it *was* time to get the hell out of here.

'So?'

'So why don't we talk about a phased-in succession plan? After all, you don't want to leave all your good work in the hands of some anonymous nobody, now do you? You want somebody you know... and can trust.'

Limace's colour changed from the usually florid to a sweaty, old wash-flannel grey, and he began to wheeze. The respiratory distress built up until he was almost choking. The Guard watched anxiously, not yet intervening; he saw all his plans go up in smoke as Limace died in front of him, his fatty coronary arteries victims of consuming rage.

He was just about to step forward (with a revolting image of potential CPR intervention in his mind's eye) when Limace's colour came suddenly back like a sunrise, from blue/grey to beyond flushed, and the wheezing took on a staccato, hiccupping quality. Veins stood out.

Lucian Limace was *laughing*. A smile spread over his suffused face. It cracked into a grin. Something had tickled him in a way that hadn't happened since he didn't know when. Maybe it was just the guileless way it was phrased, maybe it was the easy way out it afforded, but for the first time in as long as he could recall something was truly funny!

'You asshole!' he roared with laughter. 'You stinkin', useless, connivin' son of a bitch!'

Now they were both cracking up with laughter.

'I orter kick your stinkin' ass out of this building! Jeezers, Jeezers, Jeezers! I gotter give you credit. You schemin', connivin', asshole son of a bitch!'

Still laughing and wheezing, and crimson to his sweaty collar, Limace reached under his desk and hauled out a six-pack. It was never too early to celebrate.

CHAPTER SEVENTEEN

By Thursday forensic experts combing the soaked ashes of the east wing had found some remarkable clues. The fire appeared to have started on the first floor and to have spread very rapidly outwards and upwards. The melted remains of a bottle found near the entrance on the first floor proved to be of a type used for holding cleaning solvents. At the rear of the building a quantity of bottles had been found among the ashes of the security booth. These proved to be of the sort in which beer was retailed.

Painstaking reconstruction of a twisted mass of plumbing, half buried among burnt beams and floorboards, had revealed that the sprinkler valve located on the fifth floor, and serving the east side, had, indeed, been shut off, as the police chief had guessed.

There was one really strange piece of evidence, or non-evidence: every artifact in the displays on the second and third floors had apparently been consumed without trace. Even their metal fittings had evaporated.

Not every artifact. Under a pile of fallen debris in one corner of the gutted shell they had discovered a veritable time capsule. One single artifact, a mask of the Hare—N'ufnīvah, the trickster—was preserved from the fire by pure chance and antique asbestos. It was not lying where it had been exhibited, on the second floor, but on the first floor at the rear, not far from the loading bay. Strangest of all, the artifact turned out to be made of plastic. A sort of resin and fiberglass composite, as their forensic analyst had reported.

Other things that appeared to have evaporated without trace were the master keys, usually kept in the key box in the loading bay security booth. The mangled remains of the metal box had turned up, but the hooks were empty. These and many other finds were kept by the police as evidence. They were meticulously labeled and documented in a way that the museum's archaeologists would have found very familiar.

Meanwhile, eyewitnesses had been interviewed. The four security guards had recovered enough from the traumas induced by a prolonged and involuntary electric ride through the centre of town, to speak as coherently as they were normally capable. They had stuck by their story—invented by the most eloquent of them once the forklift batteries had run down—of how they had rushed from their various posts throughout the museum to the rear loading bay in response to an alarm, only to be felled by a mysterious agency. On awakening to the smell and sounds of fire they had battered their way to safety. A tissue of lies, but pinched around the snotty nose of truth.

The three policemen who had entered the building and found Bill Anker in *flagrante delicto* stated that they had come in response to a message relayed from Headquarters. Headquarters had confirmed receipt of a phone call, purportedly emanating from Museum Security.

A lonely drunk had seen a man run to a car in a back street near the museum, around the time of the fire, and drive quickly away. But who asks a lonely drunk?

The only other identified witness was Bill Anker. The chief of police had overcome his rebuff of Wednesday and had coerced a wary Anker into answering a few simple questions in the privacy of the onsite police trailer. It was simply a feeling out interview, not the taking of an official statement. He didn't want to frighten him into silence.

It had been a very strange exchange. Anker had maintained a curiously wooden demeanour and had paused at length before answering any questions. He still had his ear trouble. His story, as it was extracted piecemeal, was perfectly simple; he had arrived at the museum in response to an emergency call from a security guard, had discovered the fire, and had retreated to the front door where he was apprehended.

The chief was mystified as to why Anker had addressed him as Doris on one occasion during the interview... In contradiction to his testimony, none of the security guards would admit to phoning Anker or the City Police, even under repeated questioning.

All this added up to two things: the fire was set deliberately, and Bill Anker, by circumstantial evidence, was the one who had done it. It was almost time for the police to act.

On Thursday afternoon Director Anker sent a memo to all staff announcing an important meeting on Friday morning at 9:00 sharp. Throughout the day the staff close to Anker had noticed his distant demeanour, studied pauses, and measured speech. It wasn't like him. Although they assumed he had called this all-staff meeting, it was more accurately Doris Ironside-Anker who had called it. He had merely dictated the memo that he sent to all staff. He would take dictation and mouth her words as long as she kept him wired for sound.

That evening Anker brought home the fire safety report, and the one he had commissioned on the supposed inadequacy of the building accommodations. Doris had spent some hours studying both. He had also brought other information he considered relevant on conservation policies, artifact reproduction and display considerations but, being products of his own stumbling bureaucracy, the stuff was largely useless or misleading.

Most of the documents looked as if they had never been read, although they carried the aroma of burning, absorbed even in the safety of their filing cabinets. The sour reek hung about their living room for days.

Doris knew that no one person in the audience tomorrow would have full cognisance of all the facts, and that Anker could therefore lie himself blue in the face and get away with it. She also knew most of the Trustees personally and played bridge with Mrs Straw when she felt strong enough to stomach the shallow, mindless name-dropping conversation between rubbers. And the thin tea and micro-scopic sandwiches. Pulling the wool over their eyes, she knew, would be no challenge at all.

The main thing at this stage, she knew, was *not* to clarify. One had to inject smoke into the hall of mirrors. Cloudiness, vagueness, wide difference of opinion, conflicting facts; those were the required elements. A high level of cognitive dissonance was the aim. The classic campaign of misinformation in warfare. And business as usual in a government office.

The meeting was to take place in Building Two, the ex-bus garage, which had adequate space to house personnel displaced from the main museum building.

The contents of Anker's office had been moved here along with those of many others' because it was so close. All the corridors and any other available spaces were stacked high with cartons full of soggy, charred papers, office equipment and supplies. The rank bacon and charred wood stink of wet ash pervaded the building.

Anker arrived 15 minutes early, but museum staff had already begun to gather in the open, central portion of the building where folding chairs had been hastily set out. Most had come straight from home, and had not yet reported in to their respective buildings. The seating area was surrounded by the larger items from the collection that were too bulky to display, or didn't fit into any recognizable theme. Steam ploughing engines, huge wooden carvings, an entire apothecary's shop, and many other like and unlike items lined the walls.

It was a closed meeting. Almost all museum staff were present, but so were a few members of the Board including Mrs Straw. Somehow the chief of police had got wind of it and glowered at the back, chewing at the side of a large forefinger. On spotting him Mrs Straw had wanted him ejected, but recognizing the social implications, resorted instead to a finger-wagging directive that this was a private affair.

Rumours ran around, the meanest and most sordid of which had originated with Mutcer, who was ecstatic. He truly believed that the pressure had finally broken through and that Anker was here to announce his resignation. And if the bugger knew what was good for him, he would also nominate his successor! Mr Easel had cornered Mutcer the day before, and they had had another nice little talk.

Easel had been acting very favourably, had appeared to be very much on his side, and had promised all sorts of support. It had been a high cholesterol meeting; all butter, grease and oil, with a bit of syrup thrown in. Provided he stayed on Easel's good side, and followed the man's excellent advice, the directorship would be his! It had felt so good to be aligned with the real centre of power in this place.

When it was time, Bill Anker stepped up to the temporary podium. Museum technical services had placed a plywood box about a yard square and a foot high in front of the microphone. He always insisted on having something at least 12 inches high to stand on. He pulled the microphone down to the level of his mouth, and cleared his throat.

The murmur of conversation died, and he stood in a wide semicircle of expectant silence. He was absolutely terrified and stricken speechless. The silence hung between them as seconds ticked. At the other end of the radio link, in her car in the parking lot, Doris mistook the silence for equipment failure and shook the transceiver in anger, consigning the electronics shop and Duracell to the seventh pit of hell.

A lurid torrent of curses and abuse poured into Anker's ear, causing him to gasp, wince, and stagger back in alarm. His colour went from ashen to puce in quick succession and the audience stirred in muted approval. They didn't have any idea what was happening to him—it looked like some sort of seizure—but this was obviously going to be fun!

Doris picked up the mutter of voices as the audience stirred, ceased shaking the gadget in her hand, and began to dictate her message. Her zombie regained its composure, cocked its head on one side and waited for completion of the first sentence.

It opened its mouth and began to speak in a measured monotone like flight delays on the PA during a snowstorm.

'I have called this somewhat... Extraordinary meeting... Er... This meeting... to make an announcement... Make an announcement.'

The puppet waited, motionless, and then resumed.

'The fire in the east display galleries was, of course, a disaster... It destroyed much of the character of the museum... But there is a silver lining... It did not destroy the Treaty Bluff Collection.'

What was this? People began to sit up and take notice. A few of them knew of the deception, but were surprised at his choice of timing to reveal it. The rest wondered if he had finally taken leave of his marbles. Most thought, and secretly hoped, that he had.

The drone continued.

'No... no artifacts from the displays were destroyed... In view of the inadequate state of the building... As detailed in reports commissioned by me at various times... All the artifacts had been replaced by copies.'

His complicity in the policy of substitution was a deliberate lie— he hated the secret burden he had been landed with—but it was festooned with truth.

'The originals were removed for safekeeping... Only the copies were destroyed... The originals are safe in storage.'

The result of his revelation was sensational. A hum of talk swelled into a murmur, then a roar. A large faction was quite prepared to make him a hero on the spot. A second faction, perhaps less trusting and more informed, wondered at the ethics of what had just been revealed. Others, particularly some Board members, could remember no reports on the safety of the building, or of reproduction policies either, and were scandalized by what sounded like pure fabrication.

The chief of police sat at the back and looked thoughtful. This did not jibe with their findings at all. Their forensic people had found no evidence of any material in the vicinity of the displays that might resemble artifacts, let alone the burnt or melted plastic you might find as a residue from copies. It was their impression that the display cases had been empty, although it was hard to be sure from the ruins they were presented with. They had found just the one reproduction object, preserved from the fire by a sheet of fallen asbestos. Hmm.

Arguments broke out in the audience. Voices were raised to shouting pitch.

'Raise your hands, damn you!' bellowed Doris into the microphone. 'Stop their gabbling! Take control! You haven't finished what I want to say.'

The director staggered back again, nearly falling off the rear of the podium, and clutched at his poor ear. 'Ow, damn you, Doris! That hurts!' Recovering slowly, he held up his hands tentatively for silence. The roar continued.

'We clearly need... Ahh... Er... We need... Ow, shit, Doris! For Christ's sake turn the fucking volume down! I'm doing my best!' The noise began to subside as they noticed he apparently had more to say. They had seen his spastic jerking, but nobody seemed to have noticed the punctuated dialogue with the phantom Doris.

'It is now essential to have a new museum... There was never a better time... Better time... We need to quickly exhibit our saved artifacts... We need to turn disaster into triumph... It is my sworn duty as your director to get us a new building...'

The pandemonium resumed at greater volume. Discussion turned into shouting matches and Anker, disobeying Doris, saw his opportunity to escape. He stepped lithely off the podium, winced as his heel hit concrete, and darted as fast as he was able back to his temporary office at the rear of the building before anybody could apprehend him. He locked the door.

Mrs Straw was tearfully delighted to have the lovely things safe and sound, and in a quandary over whether Bill Anker should be castigated or congratulated. Clearly, the Board would have to be convened on an emergency basis to debate what to do. Better check and see what's in the fridge and liquor cupboard...

Very quickly, though, she became horrified with the realization that this mess might be sniffed out by the press. Publicity; the public officer's chief horror!

She stepped quickly up to the vacated podium, grabbed the microphone off its stand and swung it in front of the nearest loudspeaker. The nail-scraping shriek of feedback briefly silenced the crowd.

'I would like you all to remember,' she brayed into the relative calm, 'that the matter before you today is confidential. I am sure I do not have to remind you' (she was actually sure that she damned well did) 'of the implications of the documents you all signed as a condition of your employment. It is your duty as civil servants to uphold the highest standards of behaviour.'

This one needed a firm lid! She left the building immediately and began contacting as many Board members as she could; the sooner they met the better.

Rourke Mutcer stood at the back of the hall, seething with fury and disappointment, and swigging surreptitiously at his flask. After Easel had been to see him, things had appeared as good as they could be. He had power on his side! But now, he had fully expected a resignation, and he hadn't got it! The bald little asshole was proving more resistant than he estimated. What the hell was going on?

But he wasn't done! He determined, today, to fix Anker's wagon. He still had some ammunition left in his box, by Christ! Almost weeping with rage, he shouldered his way out of the building.

Easel was in damage-control mode. That schmuck Anker was taking all the credit and showing no signs of stepping down. He should have cracked and folded, fuck 'im! And now people knew the real artifacts were in storage, so it was goddamned essential that he, and not Anker, got all the credit! First thing to do was call Straw and give her the facts of who was really responsible. Twist her around my finger—piece of cake. He barged through the crowd and left the building. This needed control.

The chief of police sat chewing his finger amid the renewed uproar and deciding that, indeed, Anker had the motive and the means. He also noticed the behaviour of both Easel and Mutcer, and filed it somewhere in the recesses of his systematic cranium. He was so pleased he had taken a personal interest in this case; it was the most intricate he had seen for years. What a perfect way to get out of the office! But there was something larger-scale that he just wasn't getting.

The great staff meeting definitely had the effect Doris wanted. To her it resembled kicking over an anthill and watching it come to the boil like an infected pustule. (She wasn't averse to mixing metaphors, either). The whole of Personkind was buzzing with excitement over a promised new building, anger over the copy deception, relief over its revelation, respect for their new-look director, disbelief over their new-look director, contempt for their new-look director and, of course, riotous humour at all of the above. No more work was done that Friday as people stood around water coolers and photocopiers, or sat at coffee tables, arguing over the contrary things they had seen, heard and believed. Most, though, seemed to focus on the man, not on what he had said.

'I couldn't believe him! Who is this guy?'

'Sure isn't the Anker of old! My God, he made sense! Whole sentences!'

'Yeah, that's right. But kind of mechanical. You think he's on drugs?'

'Might be. Whatever helps, because he couldn't get any worse.' This from a laconic admin assistant who had seen him at his most dilatory.

'Tell me about it! You should have been at the conference last weekend,' interjected a junior researcher, coffee cup in hand. 'He gave this paper on museum administration and, honest to God, nobody could understand a single word. It was, like, gobble-dee-gook!'

'Yeah, but that was just some of that business-speak, wasn't it?'

'No, not this stuff. We've all read that re-org crap, but his stuff was *really* off the wall!'

'What was the reaction? With the delegates?'

'That's the funny bit. They were embarrassed or confused or... I dunno... stunned. So, they hardly moved, and nobody said a word at the end. Except old Horn-Parforce, of course. He was the session chair. Syrupy old fart!'

Tonight was the museum dinner, a fixture in the institute's calendar. Even with the main building reduced to ashes and rubble, the museum dinner must go on. They might not have a museum, but nobody was going to take away their damned dinner! This was another glittering soirée when all staff and their spouses, the Board of Trustees and even the minister and his escort and handlers would gather to eat, drink, dance, socialize, and listen with half an ear to speeches.

This was the one occasion in the year when staff who normally despised each other would chat amiably, enquiring after each other's welfare and gathering dirt for later use, like the best of friends. Mildly drunk employees of the lower echelons could talk wittily to members of the Board, curator's wives could condescend to cleaners, and even old Caliban could be coaxed into uttering nearly complete sentences. People looked forward to this wondrous soiree for months and no fire or flood or third world war would get in its way.

The ballroom of the museum, normally reserved for such grand occasions, was blackened brick and stinking ashes. The museum dinner would be held in Building Two, in the same location as the all-staff meeting. It was the only building that had enough space to seat all staff in comfort.

A few of the larger museum objects had to be shifted aside, enlarging the space already created for the morning's meeting, and some shelving had to be moved as well. By late afternoon it had become a fit place for the banquet, especially when the furniture rental firm and the caterers had done their stuff. Even the redolence of recent fire was partially masked by the smell of freshly cut fir and spruce.

The stimulation of the morning's meeting resulted in action on several fronts. Over the next few hours Anker, Mutcer, Easel, Caliban, Tort, Straw, Indoda Enhle, and the chief of police would weave a curious ballet, culminating in a grand finale this very night, at the museum dinner.

Chapter Eighteen

No matter how well the switch had been done, the thieves could not possibly have left things exactly as they found them. The conservation staff would naturally have their suspicions aroused if even the slightest change in the wellbeing or disposition of their babies was noticed.

Stephanie Chang's senses had been alerted as soon she went back to work after the all-staff meeting in Building Two. At first, she had thought somebody had been in the storage area poking around and looking it over. Perhaps the security guard? There were small indications of disturbance—a curtain not pulled back here, a corner of foam padding not tucked in just so, slightly misaligned Velcro tie-backs—and as a conservator she was an attentive stickler for detail. It was her profession, and her predisposition.

Then, while checking the Treaty Bluff storage racks she detected a hint of cloying, sickly sweet peppermint. It emanated from a carved wooden mask of E'man'ekaf, the nightmare man of the woods. As she looked closer, she noticed the absence of an accession number. The accession number is a vital part of the documentation of a museum piece. Somewhere on the object, usually in an unobtrusive place, one will always find a small, unique number. Some fool in Registration must have forgotten to apply it. A conservator wouldn't be so careless. Or, to be fair, perhaps it had rubbed or abraded off. But, wait a minute! Something was very odd here!

The copies were fantastically accurate, but when Stephanie couldn't find the number, she picked the mask up to turn it over, and was struck with puzzlement. It just didn't feel right. Her experience with the handling of materials, so much more finely tuned than the rusty skills of many a Personkind curator, warned her that something was amiss.

As she exposed the underside of the mask she jumped back in horror and almost dropped it. There was a huge blob of what looked like chewing gum stuck to the inside surface! Grabbing a stainless-steel probe, she began levering the grey, peppermint-scented mass away. It was, indeed, chewing gum, and evidently the result of a recent inept repair. The gum, still sticky and aromatic, couldn't have been there for more than a few days. (Having worked on a row of historic seats from the old Regency Theatre, Stephanie knew what old chewing gum looked like.) Worse was to come. As she peeled the reluctant blob away from the surface, a gaping stab wound with torn edges was revealed, apparently made with a sharp object like a knife. And bursting forth from the hole was not splintered wood, but shredded fiberglass. It was one of the copies!

E'man'ekaf was breeding his nightmares again.

Easel came quickly to the storage area as soon as Stephanie informed him. He examined the piece himself, came to the same conclusion, and looked at her in a wholly new way that frightened her. Her eyes slid away from his; he made her feel guilty and scared, but she didn't know why. She was only the messenger. There was some-thing about his eyes...

'This dunt match with the fax,' he observed cryptically.

She wanted to tell him of her suspicions. She wanted to tell him of her sense that the storage area had been disturbed.

'You know what I think...' she began.

'I'm not inneressid in what you think,' he cut in, pushing her aside. 'Stan' back and lemme look!'

She stepped aside, hurt and rebuffed.

He quickly removed other objects from adjacent shelves and came to the same baffling conclusion. There were gouged marks in the backs of some, and no numbers! Not a fuckin' accession number! His brain reeling, his control wavering, Easel stamped off immediately to his office and phoned Caliban, who made his way to Building Four from his reproductions studio in Building Three, several blocks away.

It was an unholy alliance; Caliban hated Easel because of the un-happiness he spread around him, but saw him as the source of all the success of his department, while Easel hated Caliban because he was foreign and talked funny, but he had needed him to further his great plans. Ten minutes of anxiety passed—Stephanie silent in the back-ground, Easel pulling objects out and cursing—before the old Czech shuffled into the storage area, emitting huge clouds of smoke.

'Put that fuckin' thing out in here! You're a fire hazard and you're breakin' the lor. Now, come 'n' looka this.'

'Ah, yers, is all epoxy fiberglass jee zers crize,' Caliban confirmed. 'Is all by me makit plastic years and years.' He coughed tearingly.

'Jew mean they're all goddam idennical fakes?' shouted Easel. His brain was trying to balance known fact with known falsehood, failing to reconcile the two, and threatening overload.

'Is no usèd fake, no no no, is copy good make. World best. No usèd trying fool nobody, no, no, no, jee zers buggering crize!'

They weren't fakes! Why did people keep saying these things were fakes, when they were absolutely the best copies anybody could make? Had he been able to read the display labels, which made no reference to the fact that the viewer was seeing a reproduction not the real thing, or to converse with the curatorial or conservation staff on their own ground, he would have discovered the huge fraud that had been perpetrated all these years, of which he was an unwitting instrument and accomplice. But he lived in a demarcated Czech language world of his own devising and such opportunities never presented themselves.

They checked another piece, then more and more. Stephanie remained in the background, ignored while the crisis dominated their attention, and glad to be out of Easel's focus while this evil mood was on him. She, too, could not understand what was happening. It was more than mystifying. It was supernatural. She was scared.

'What the hell is this? Woss goin' on here?' Easel barked at Caliban almost rhetorically as they examined yet another piece.

'Is not all copy in display put? Here real thing only?'

Caliban only appears naïve because of his imperfect hold on the English language, and thus his total inability to grasp the nuances behind the mere words. Nevertheless, he knew evil when he met it, and people like Easel set off alarms at the subconscious level that transcends language. And this apparent substitution scared him; years ago, even less in touch with others than he was now, he had been coerced by Mutcer—and Anker too—to do something he didn't really approve of; make a second copy from an original mold. But at that time, he was even less cognizant of the interplay of the characters in this drama than he was now. Still, his complicity worried him, the substitution baffled him, Easel frightened him, and he just wished he could get a chance to set the record straight.

Finally, Easel stood back, desperately trying to evoke an image of calm and order in front of his inferiors, while only just maintaining control of the riot of thoughts in his head. To see Easel nonplussed was to understand the true extent of the mystery. From his craftiness in bending Mrs Straw's ear, soiling Anker's reputation and taking credit for the copies, he was now turned 180 degrees into confusion. Here were the copies! Where were the originals?

He was seething inside, but had absolutely no direction in which to turn it. Something was going to get smashed. It was a pity he didn't have an old-timer's hockey game tonight, because it would be surprising if somebody on the opposing team didn't end up in hospital. Or somebody on his team for that matter.

'We better tell Egg 'Ead,' he sighed, realizing that there, at least, he could find someone to bully and threaten.

Now the worst appeared to be over for the director. He had won a huge concession from Doris; he would not be obliged to speak at the museum dinner tonight. In truth, his voice was a little scratchy—and he feared it might get worse—but his fear of public speaking, and rumours trickling back about his performance at the conference, were what really clinched it. He found Doris to be surprisingly compliant, perhaps because she sympathized with the pressure she had put him under, but more likely because she didn't trust him to speak without her dictation, which would be impossible, of course, with her sitting right there at the same table.

He had phoned Mrs Straw, who was acting as emcee, and told her of his developing 'laryngitis.' She had sounded distant and cold. He had no idea why; he thought she would be delighted at the turn of events. Then, with his usual gift for making the wrong decision, he had suggested that W. W. Easel—perhaps the ugliest exponent of the English language at large in the museum—give a talk in his place. As it happened, Easel had something on conservation already prepared, which would doubtless have the audience riveted to their chairs.

In the relative calm Anker's controller considered it safe to break radio contact with him for a while. Strangely enough, he had been getting used to it, although he did have a habit of speaking to himself occasionally and it was a little vexing to have a tiny, disembodied voice in his ear asking him what the hell he was talking about.

Still, a bit of peace from that annoyance helped him savour what, at this point, felt like the beginnings of better times. The artifacts safe, a new facility on the horizon, things could be worse.

The phone destroyed his peace.

'You better get over here quick!' said the tense voice of the chief of Conservation. 'There's somethin' you gotta see.'

Little alarm bells rang in the region of his gall bladder and his shit-on-the-horizon detector was beeping yet again. He felt his new optimism fold and crumble like a burning paper party hat.

He pulled his coat on hurriedly and rushed the few blocks from

Building Two to the conservation labs and storage area. He arrived out of breath and damp from sleet.

'All the artifax in storage from the displays are fakes,' blurted Easel as soon as Anker entered the foyer. 'All fakes! Every one of 'em!' He cocked his head in the direction of Caliban. ''E knows.'

'Yers, is all usèd bolyester fiberglass epoxy madit,' wheezed the old Czech, quite infected with the tension, but all oblivious of the implications. 'But is no fakes, no, no, shit no!'

Anker stood, dumbly uncomprehending.

Easel leant into his face and hissed, below the old Czech's threshold of hearing as he was into one of his periodic fits of coughing:

'I need some fuckin' answers from you. You better come and see what's what. If you've had them pieces switched without me knowing... You wait, I'll get you! Jus' watch your fuckin' back!'

He turned and went into the storage area, Anker trailing behind.

Tonight was the museum dinner.

Later that afternoon, once he had returned from examining the plastic reproductions with Easel and Caliban, Anker sat at his desk appallingly dejected and miserable. What in God's name was going on? He ticked off supposed facts in his mind:

One: he knew the objects in the displays had all been reproductions. How could they not have been, when it was one of his worst causes of anxiety, and the museum's most horrible secret?

Two: if the objects in the museum were repros, then those in storage in Building Four *had* to be original.

Three: they weren't.

Four: then the ones on display were.

Five: so the real ones had got torched.

Six: who did the switch?

Seven: when?

Eight: why?

Nine: how?

Ten: oh, damn, my head's spinning.

There was no eleven...

A knock sounded at the door as Pork Mutcer waltzed in without waiting and perched his gamy posterior on the corner of the desk. He'd now had his fill of subtle threats and innuendos. He was furious that Anker had apparently stumbled through the present mess on his feet. Now was the time to turn up the heat... and talk about fires.

But first, a little diversion while he deployed his other hoarded secret weapon.

'Yes, Mr Mutcer, what can I do for you?' He hated using the man's first name. It symbolized an intimacy that he shunned. He wished he'd kept the door locked.

'Does the name Lionel mean anything to you?' Mutcer asked with a guileless innocence quite out of character.

Of course it did, although he was mystified as to why Mutcer had raised the subject.

'No, not especially,' he lied warily. 'Why do you ask?'

'Oh, just that, a few years ago a certain Lionel wrote you. Lavender envelope, flowery notepaper, and not exactly subtle with what he said either. Do your kind of men really do that sort of thing to each other?'

Anker remembered the letters from Lionel Rolling-Stock and began to be filled with a welling sense of horror. He broke into a sweat. He recalled one letter in particular; and having being shocked at what the old man had implied and suggested. He had written back immediately setting him straight (if that's the right word). Anker had destroyed the letter—he *knew* he had—so what was all this about? How could Mutcer know about any of this? It was all so long ago!

'What are you implying? What are you trying to say?' he asked warily.

'Simply that that letter…'

'I don't know what you're talking about!' interrupted Anker, now getting thoroughly scared and flustered. 'I don't know anything about any letter.'

'…which happened to land in my mail slot by mistake one day. I couldn't resist gently opening it. He must have a really dry tongue, but I'm sure you would know all about that. And then I made a copy.'

He waved a piece of paper he had extracted from an inner pocket.

'Anybody who sends letters through the post in lavender envelopes is just asking for trouble, don't you think?'

Anker was terrified and embarrassed. This was horrible! Unreal! Doris would kill him!

'No, no! You don't understand! That letter was a huge mistake. He didn't mean any of it! He retracted it all. I wrote back to him and told him. It was all a mistake!'

'Got a copy of your reply? No? Pity. Without it, things do look a little… ah… queer, don't they?'

'Give me that copy! Give it back! You're evil! Evil!'

'Evil?' said Mutcer quietly, folding the paper and returning it to its fetid hiding place. 'No, I'm not evil. I'm just using the tools I have to use to get what I want.'

There was an irony, lost on both of them, in the tool himself using tools.

'You are deliberately making up lies about me!'

'Lies? Who says they're lies? Just you. It's only your word against everybody else's. People believe what they want to believe. And every time you and old Lionel appear at the same functions it's all buddy-buddy. Even going to bars with him. Don't think people haven't noticed.'

'You... you...' spluttered Anker, almost speechless with anger and horror. 'What... what do you want?'

Mutcer decided to go in for the one-two punch. 'I want your job. So there's something you can do for me, *Bill*. Something nobody else can do.'

Anker was trying to regain composure, trying to think, and being visited by nightmare scenarios of his whole world crashing down. Doris! She wouldn't believe it. No. Would she? Would she? Circumstantial evidence? Oh, Christ! No, no, don't even go there!

'Do for you?' he gurgled.

By good fortune Doris had chosen this moment to resume communication after a bout of shopping. On her way home she had pulled over into a parking lot near the building, got out the electronic gizmo and switched on. It was her intention to tell him she was going home and to remind him to leave enough time to get dressed for the museum dinner. She was bored and tired and not particularly enamoured of this stupid caper with her hopeless husband and the web of lies, subterfuge, hidden agendas, and fabrications that he had allowed to surround him.

'...yes, do for me, Bill,' she caught. Her ears immediately pricked up. 'Fact is, old boy, you can get out of my way! I've just about had it with beating about the bush. I am going to be director, and we'll have a new museum, and you are not going to stop me!'

Doris quickly got back in the saddle.

'If you think,' she dictated, 'that you can browbeat me...' but she got no further. What came out of her husband's mouth was an incoherent mumble with only the word 'browbeat' discernible.

'Shut up and listen to me, you stupid jerk! Your private life's one thing. But you know damned well you're covering up the destruction of that mask! And you know I've got all the documentation we produced on it, safely tucked away with your signature all over it. Your signature, my silence, remember? That was the deal.'

He looked reflectively at the ceiling, mercurial in his changes of mood, recalling images from the past.

'Ye-es, remember how you wanted to check the textile parts on that Hare mask? And you put a match to a tiny strand, eh? The standard test for wool? Careless with the matches, eh? Remember how it roared up in flames. Lucky it was in the fume hood, eh? But it was too late, wasn't it, *Billy?* Totally destroyed. Not even Easel found out, and he had done the treatment! Nitro-cellulose, the fucking fool! And then we discovered all those years of Caliban's fakery. What a godsend! Bribing the old goat to make another from the same mould! Jee-zers-crize. Two fakes; no vulcanized original! I've even got the canceled cheque you gave him to shut him up! I cashed it for him!' he roared with horrible brittle, sick laughter.

So, this was her dearest's true secret! Dear God, the cretin's gone and let that toad Mutcer get a lever on him! Is there no end to this mess? And why the hell didn't he tell me? I suppose he thinks I'm like all the others; that I can't be trusted. Well, I'll make the bugger trust me, if I have to thump it into him. Jesus, Daddy, maybe you were right all along!

Doris decided to sit back and let the smelly chief curator incriminate himself. This clinched it. He was definitely bananas. Then again, he did work for Bill...

'I've got you, *William*. If you don't step down and nominate me for your job, the whole truth will come out. One fire in your past is bad enough. Add that to the cover-up. What will they think of all the other circumstantial evidence? Limace's report that tells you exactly where the sprinkler shutoff is. Eh? That long-nosed cop knows what's going on. And my good friend Mr Easel? What if he found out about the mask? Dangerous, he is. One word from me, and you are in the doo-doo. Do it my way, or they'll have your ass.

'You quit,' he concluded nastily, 'or the excrement hits the ventilator. I'll see you tomorrow to hear your decision. Sweetie.'

'Right!' said the little voice in Anker's ear. 'We have things to talk about, do we not?' and cut the connection. Anker slid further into his miserable dejection and the absence of the little voice in his ear didn't exactly lighten his mood. Until this moment had no idea that his dejection and misery could get any worse. Doris pulled out of the parking lot and headed home.

Tonight was the museum dinner.

Later again the same day. Evening was falling and cool winds played with stained, drifted snow. A cold wetness clogged the spirit. Having abandoned her listening post, Doris returned home to dress and make up for the evening's festivities. Her brain was seething with ideas, but also boiling with frustration. Things were spinning beyond control, and it seemed as if her dear museum director was dancing an off-balance polka on slimy, rotten boards over the septic tank that his incompetence and inattention had constructed beneath his feet.

Got to do something!

The man himself was beyond constructive thought, negative or otherwise. He was feeling lonely and dejected. Winter was blowing through his brain. He ought to get up the energy and go home. Things couldn't get worse, surely.

Another knock at the door.

Lana Straw entered the office rather diffidently and shook hands with much less than her usual warmth. She sat carefully, addressed him in a neutral voice and sounded as if she had studied and memorized her words.

'This morning, I convened an emergency meeting of the Board of Trustees to consider recent events in and around the museum. Although the Board is unable to satisfy itself on the many points at issue, it feels that you, as director of the institution, have acted in a less-than-professional fashion. Although no decision has been made, the Board feels it necessary to convene an inquiry into all this confusing activity, in which you seem to be a major player. You are requested to step down as director effective tomorrow morning until the enquiry has been completed and recommendations drawn up. You will occupy the temporary position of special advisor.

'I'm sorry Bill,' she concluded quietly. 'It's the Board's decision, not mine.'

When she left, the room felt very empty.

But not for long.

The chief of police, accompanied by Sergeant Delios with his note pad and pencil, entered the office scarcely 10 minutes after Mrs Straw had left. They didn't even bloody knock, let alone wait to be called in.

The chief plunked himself down in a chair without being asked, while the sergeant stood near the door.

'Oh, Christ! Not another visitation!' wailed Anker. 'What're you? The Ghost of Shit-Yet-To-Come?'

'Hmm. Our investigations are now nearly completed. There is no question concerning the cause of the fire. It was arson. A fire deliberately set in the first-floor display area while the sprinklers for that side of the building had been shut off. The place where the fire started was near where you were discovered by the police. The security guards on duty that night have sworn under oath that you were not phoned at home by them. We have their statements. In view of the seriousness of the situation, we feel it wise at this stage to take a written statement from you. First, I must remind you of your rights...'

Tonight was the museum dinner!

CHAPTER NINETEEN

I t was a wonderful meal. This near Christmas, the decorations were festive and carried the themes of holly and mistletoe and snow. Paper festoons and balloons hung from the walls, from the shelves of artifacts, and even from the smokestack of one of the steam ploughing engines.

The caterers and rental people had done a lovely job, transforming the vast storage space by cunning lighting into an intimate boudoir, and providing a meal fit for such opulent surroundings. There was a head table across the narrow end of the room, with three others extending from it, thus forming an attenuated E. Down the centre of each table candles in elaborate holders lit the sparkling silver and glassware. There was sherry to start with, then a bottle of wine to every four guests, with more to come. Liqueurs and brandy were a promise for the near future. Mock turtle soup was followed by a garden salad; the entrées were roast beef or *coq au vin*, and for dessert there was a choice of cheesecake or cherries jubilee.

At the rear of the room, behind the head table, a quintet of string players scrubbed industriously, evoking images of velvet breeched and periwigged musicians of a bygone era. It was Mrs Straw's insistence that all such occasions should have the 'right kind' of music. She used her influence with the musical community of the city to ensure this every year. Symphonic players who loved to jam with their friends were co-opted into making trios, quartets and bigger ensembles as the occasion demanded. The museum dinner was only one of many venues. So, they would whale away at the classics, fading into the background during speeches or presentations, and wading back in again when silence threatened to fall, as though reacting to an acoustic *horror vacuii*.

As the guests were milling around the tables, smacking their lips over the last dregs of a flamboyantly and falsely labelled cooking sherry, and trying to find their places, the quintet was solidly into Schubert's C Major (and irritating Charles Orville Jones exceedingly by using two violas instead of two cellos).

It did strike some people—especially Indoda Enhle, who was there as an honoured guest—as rather odd that music played in Vienna two or more centuries ago was considered the 'right kind' in an ambience of native arts and culture. Then again, in the dinosaur environment of this museum, anthropology, ethnology, and like disciplines were driven relentlessly by WASP agendas. It reminded him of the Ghanaian music student from the University in Legon who was studying ethnomusicology by writing his thesis on Beethoven's quartets.

The hierarchy of the museum topped by the minister attended in condescending order. Museum staff and their other halves were in abundance, and the guest list also included the chief of police. The chief wasn't quite sure why he had been invited, but it was a free meal with lots of booze, so why turn it down? This was not true for Indoda Enhle. As an influential champion of cultural causes, it was always considered wise, polite and politic to invite him to the dinner. He was thoroughly enjoying the hospitality, but having occasional bouts of concern over that visitation of the protesters, and the things their visit implied.

Doris Ironside-Anker occupied a key place at the head table where she could hobnob with the Almighty, in the shape of the minister of Culture and Professional Sport. Her strategy had been to engage the minister in a conversation on culture and heritage, thus getting an idea of where he stood on key issues of museum development, funding and infrastructure. Particularly funding. This proved a futile ploy because it turned out that, upon pumping the man, he was an empty vessel. He was filled by his aides only moments before Question Period or functions more official than this one. He filed what he needed to repeat into his short-term memory like an art history student cramming for a slide test, and quickly voided the memory when the task was done. Only the words 'going forward' remained. As this was one of his 'free' days he knew absolutely nothing, and cared even less. Doris was able to hold a conversation of several sentences with him on the slim chances of the local football team, going forward, but that was all.

Bill Anker was on the minister's other side, in a central position. With Doris present the radio link was necessarily discontinued. He was a mess of conflicting internal emotions and external twitches and tremors. Memories, consequences, and future scenarios flooded his mind. He had been so optimistic earlier that day, but everything had crashed and burned. He *wanted* to enjoy the museum dinner, the highlight of the year, but he just *couldn't*. Thank God, at least, that he wouldn't have to stand up and speak. That was Easel's task.

Rourke Mutcer also had a place at the head table in his role of chief curator. At previous museum dinners he had tried the old crowded bus expedient of blaming his porky tang on those around him, but it was senseless to continue this strategy, as everybody now knew the culprit. In fact, there was a vicious competition when table seatings were being decided as far back as September to avoid being placed next to him. 'Look,' as C. O. Jones observed, 'even the friggin' silverware turns black in front of him.' Jones's wife agreed wholeheartedly. She had been stuck next to him two years running and suspected collusion. Mutcer had allayed the issue somewhat by using a powerful deodorant. It was supplied by a veterinary friend, and was prescribed for large dogs with terrible farts. He also took frequent nips at his flask, which lent him a spiritual aura.

Desserts had been stowed away and guests were topping off their sherry and two or three wines with a round of liqueurs. Rumbling and belching contentedly, they settled deeper into their chairs, the better to tolerate the obligatory speechifying; the duckbilled platitudes that completed the sit-down phase of the evening. Things began with a deadly, ghostwritten speech by the minister—who betrayed his utter indifference to the topic by reading in sentence bites from a piece of paper—followed by a few saccharine, but mercifully quick, noises from Chairperson and emcee Mrs Straw. She then apologized for the director's laryngitis, and proffered an invitation to Mr Easel to take the podium.

Easel rose to his hind legs. His mind was a riot of confusion over the earlier discovery, but he hoped giving the speech would push it all, at least temporarily, into the background.

'Thankew laze 'n' gem.' He put down his glass, shuffled his papers and continued, 'I dislike to say...'

His audience were at first astonished at both his candour and his rudeness, before they slowly cottoned to his imperfect diction and realized that he was trying to form the words 'I would just like to say...' From then on it was plain sailing; they just ignored almost every word he uttered.

'I dislike to say how please I am t'be given this apperchoony [opportunity: two Ts, almost impossible.] ...apperchoony t'dress this occaishn. Bein' the cenner of attenshn I feel like a penis before a big recile...'

Ears perked a little, eyebrows rose a fraction, then they subsided again. The string quintet whined away unobtrusively in the background. Easel whined away obtrusively in the foreground. It was all so excruciatingly dull: the ugly droning voice and the sobbing strings. The uneasy balance maintained by gastric elasticity stretched to its limits by too much dessert, and the boozy swimming ambience derived from virtually bottomless carafes of wine, sherry and brandy, blended into a giddy, swirling continuum.

People prayed for something to liven it up...

That same evening, Sue Tort and Terry O'Weight were preparing the next stage of their campaign of repatriation. She paced the sticky vinyl tiles of their rented accommodation.

'Aw right, no more middlemen! That was a complete fuck up!'

'Yeah,' agreed O'Weight. 'How were *we* to know they were copies? Shit!'

'An' it won't help if we show up again with the real McCoy. He'll still be pissed at us. You'd expect a bit of gratitude, wouldn't you?'

'Yeah, we're doing all this for them. Stealing an' that. I just don't get it.'

'How many times do I hafta tell you it's not stealing? It's called liberation!'

She sighed. Sometimes...

'Anyways,' she continued, 'this time we go straight to the source. They're having their goddamned museum dinner tonight in the temporary building. Building Two. What better audience could we have? We just step in an' tell the pigged out, swilling crowd we've got the stuff and they better start negotiating, or else. Merry fuckin' Christmas! Let's go down to our good ole rental truck and choose something to show them, prove we mean business!'

There had been a discrepancy in their auditing. After their second burglary they had one artifact extra in the haul. It was the mask of the Hare: N'ufnīvah. O'Weight remembered removing the 'original' from its display case during the burglary of the museum displays, but could not remember having packed it in the truck. It was not recorded on the Carpenter's inventory either. Now, after the second burglary, its twin had turned up. This was a mystery that he could not really cope with because his brain, you see, was just three sizes too small.

Meanwhile, the police had the identical Hare as part of their forensic evidence: the one found preserved miraculously from the fire. It had proved to be made of plastic; epoxy resin and fiberglass. Two copies, no original. Anker and Mutcer had watched the original go up in flames years ago.

Of all possible artifacts in the liberated collection, it was the mask of the Hare—Bill Anker's nemesis—that O'Weight chose as the emissary of their intentions. It was the only copy among the whole lot! N'ufnīvah! You really are the trickster, aren't you?

They climbed into their rental truck and drove to Building Two. Their liberated goods were left in the back, but O'Weight carried the Hare in a blanket on his lap. Tort decided not to stop in the parking lot between Building Two and the main museum, but on the street around the other side. She considered it less likely to attract notice, and if all else failed she figured they could make a quicker getaway. O'Weight stayed in the driver's seat of the truck—Tort didn't want him around for this—while she carried the mask, still shrouded, up the backstairs and into the banqueting chamber.

Just at the point when boozed employees were sick and tired of Easel's voice, and wished to God they had the guts, even from a position of anonymity, to tell him to shut the fuck up and sit down, or hurl a bread roll at his head, a disturbance at the back of the room answered their prayers. Heads turned as everybody craned to see what the commotion was all about.

Sue Tort pushed a caterer aside and strode into the room carrying the unveiled mask before her. When Anker saw it he blanched. Disbelief turned to horror and he broke into an awful sweat. He was transfixed with a paralyzing wave of terror and confusion. Of all the places and all the times to have his crime brought into the open! But who was she? Why her? And where did she get it? He stared uncomprehendingly as she strode round to the head table and began to speak.

'Aw right! Lissen everybody! Lissen careful! We're fighting for the repatriation of these people's artifacts. All their stuff in your storage? The stuff that got saved from the fire? It's all fakes! We've got all the original stuff in hiding. Safe. And unless you cooperate, you'll never see it again! Any of it!

'This,' and she held the Hare high above her head, 'is proof of our intentions! The real thing!'

A roar of startled conversation broke out. This was a delightful little intermezzo! As she held N'ufnīvah aloft, though, the noise died down slowly to a murmur, and then silence. The string quintet wailed into stillness. The tension could be measured in thousands of Newtons.

It was broken by an ancient wheezing voice from one side of the head table.

'Ahh, no no no, is from plastic makit years and years. I usèd make zis epoxy fiberglass jee zers crize, yes yes.'

She whirled to identify the voice, momentarily unsure of herself. The word 'fiberglass' had given her a rush of shit to the heart.

168

'Whadda you mean? What? Who are you?'

With a sudden flash of insight Bill Anker saw salvation. He saw angels and heard trumpets. He was vouchsafed a holy vision. He realized what was happening, what had happened, and what would happen in a parallel, integrated way that his poor brain could never normally encompass. It was naked intuition. Suddenly it all made sense! Taking the future of his career in both hands, he leapt to his feet and ignoring his 'laryngitis,' he yelled.

'Sure it's plastic! Sure, it's a fake! They *all* are!' he lied.

Tort's face underwent terrible transformations.

'*No, no, no!*' she screamed. 'We've got the originals!'

'Test it!' Anker yelled. 'Go on! Test it!' He had nothing to lose. He knew it was false! He'd been there when the original exploded in flames.

She seized a dirty fork from the table in front of her and dug it violently into the mask. Fiberglass burst out in shreds as the fork buried itself. She screamed loudly, hurled the Hare down the length of the table, and burst into shrieking tears.

N'ufnīvah thundered along through bowls of discarded cherries jubilee, knocked over brandy snifters and wine bottles, and settled itself in front of Indoda Enhle, who had been sitting astonished and fascinated at this unfolding theatre. He rose to his feet and Tort spotted him through her tears.

'*You!*' she shrieked.

'*You!*' he roared.

He was on his chair, and onto the table and ploughing through the remains of the feast before she could move. He scooped up handfuls of rented cutlery and began hurling knives, forks and spoons at her like the man in the circus as she bolted for the rear exit. Whooping and bellowing he leapt from the table, clawed his way past distracted diners, and chased her out of the exit and down the stairs. Anker, realizing that the lost artifacts were in her hands, passed quickly though the door and followed the trail of damaged cutlery.

Tort ran to the truck in the street, climbed in sobbing and screaming and locked the door. Indoda Enhle, with Anker on his heels, grabbed on to the truck's wing mirror and tried to open the passenger door. Anker went round to the driver's side and hauled on the door handle. Beating Anker away from his door, trying to get the truck moving, and trying to find out what the hell had gone wrong, occupied O'Weight for some seconds. Finally, the truck rolled forward with Anker and Indoda Enhle still hanging grimly onto either side.

169

Meanwhile, Easel, furious at being interrupted in the middle of his discourse, and by now completely overwhelmed in contradictory information, finally snapped. He saw and felt a roaring red flood in front of his eyes. Unable to attack Anker, the centre of his hatred and loathing and confusion, he grabbed the nearest likely victim at one of the side tables and pulled his shirt over his head preparatory to pummeling him. He even made the arms-down, shake-off gesture of dropping imaginary hockey gloves before grabbing him.

His victim was Brian Connolly, who had come to the museum dinner as Stephanie Chang's somewhat reluctant guest. (Frankly, they hadn't been getting on as well as she hoped they would. She wanted more; he seemed content with dancing the old box spring tango every night. Apart from that, all he would talk about was his bloody car. Things were strained.)

On seeing young Stephanie's man in trouble, Caliban, who was seated next to them, seized a bottle close at hand, stepped around the end of the table and, reaching on tiptoe from behind, brought it down on Easel's head. It was full and it knocked him cold. As he began to collapse, Brian got his head clear of his shirt and—no gentleman he, and delighted at the opportunity to strike a blow against the museum—brought his knee up and rang the Christmas bells for joy.

'Is nobugger do dat people Christmas jee zers crize,' rumbled Caliban as a stunned Easel slid half under the table.

With the party now in complete bedlam, guests screaming and yelling, shattered crockery and squashed food littering the floor, the string quintet decided to saw valiantly on as heroically as the band on the *Titanic*.

Mutcer saw his moment. Amid strains of *Nearer My God to Thee* he stepped forward to the microphone. He had judged his moment well; if he could calm the crowd and blacken his absent director in one motion, he would have won the day. But Doris foresaw his intention and acted almost as quickly as he did.

'Your valiant director...' he had only just begun in a loud voice, when a massive hip check caught him in the side and pinned him gasping to the edge of the table. It would have got her a standing-O in any hockey game. The hip flask in his back pocket took the full force and buckled and burst. Strong spirits soaked his pants and shot out in a wide spray. Too close to the candles!

A loud *whoof!* A great sheet of blue flame tinged with yellow shot from the clothing in Mutcer's nether regions, roaring the length of the head table, igniting overturned brandy snifters with muffled detonations and turning the paper tablecloth into an incandescent carpet.

'He's gone and done it again!' bellowed Doris in an access of inspiration that matched her husband's. 'First the museum, now this! The man's a fire hazard! *Arson! Arson!*'

Yelling in terror and suffering the agonies of Edward II, Mutcer hurled himself through the mob in the direction of the front door with Doris in hot pursuit. She grabbed a heavy weapon in the form of a full champagne bottle from the table as she passed. The heat of the blazing feast set the fire alarms ringing and melted the fusible plugs in the sprinklers. Panic-stricken guests, choking on the unaccustomed fumes of red-hot cherries jubilee, brandy at flashpoint and blazing tablecloths, were incontinently deluged with freezing, rusty water. The string quintet wailed down into silence for the final time.

Doris followed her quarry through the main doors by the white flash of his exposed backside where most of his lower clothing had been burnt away. He dashed out into the parking lot, some distance ahead of her, and had his car started and moving before she could close with him. As the car sped forward, she hurled herself onto the hood, grabbing onto one of the wipers, and pounded at the windshield with her champagne bottle until both exploded in foam and glistening fragments. She reached in through the starred aperture, rending her evening dress from neck to waistline and spilling great volumes of white bosom, and grabbed Mutcer around the throat. The grip on his windpipe and the vision before his eyes made him lose control of himself and his vehicle.

The car tore around the corner of the building, almost on two wheels, down a slope into the street, and ploughed head-on into the rented truck tearing in the opposite direction. Anker and his wife met each other in the most unexpected circumstances, miraculously not badly hurt, amid the ruins of Pork's car.

Indoda Enhle sprawled briefly in the road with a wing mirror clutched in his hand before leaping up and chasing the activists, who were running for it in terror. All three went howling and yelling down a side street away from Building Two.

Anker went quickly to the rear of the truck, opened the door and openly cried with happiness and relief when he found the carefully wrapped collection.

Doris rose to her feet, hauled the weakly protesting Mutcer out of the wreckage and began pummeling him with a torn-off windshield wiper.

'I'll maim you, you vermin! You filth! I'll dance on yer giblets! I'll do a hornpipe on yer wedding tackle! I'll flog the bowels out of yer back, you scum, you garbage, you offal, you bastard spawn of Satan!'

A golden glow of extreme wellbeing emanating from the pit of her stomach suffused her, and she continued the pummeling.

Finally, his cries for mercy and the passing of the peak of her satisfaction caused her to desist.

'Mercy! Anything! Mercy! I'll do anything!' he gasped, caught in a terrible Visegrip® midway between pain and pleasure. 'Mercy! No! Stoppit! *Help!*'

'Anything? All right!' She flung him aside on the tarmac like a bag of rancid kitchen scraps. 'I'll deal with you later. Now get up, and piss off!'

The soaked and choking partygoers streaming out of the steaming building were just in time to witness the full capitulation.

CHAPTER TWENTY

I t was Sunday, two evenings after the museum dinner, and it was Doris's bridge night with Mrs Straw and two other ladies of the Board of Trustees. They played regularly at the Straw mansion; her old man was a wheel in a law firm and spent ostentatiously. It was a venue for conversation and point scoring, for tea from fine, thin, floral-patterned china, and for the presentation of genteel sandwiches cut with a microtome, which were never big enough to give you the impression you might actually be eating.

On this occasion Doris was greeted in the foyer of the great house with less than the usual cordiality. There had been a coldness on the phone earlier in the evening when she had confirmed their date, and stated in no uncertain terms that she would be there with bells on. Mrs Straw would have preferred to just do a little knitting, or bring in a substitute.

Doris made a fourth with the bridge bitches for purely political reasons. She had been able to steer some far-reaching decisions on museum policy and administration just by biding her time, sensing her moment, and making just the right move. Bit like bridge really. And now, her long-suffering auditions of the multifarious faults and shortcomings of everybody except the one who was at the moment holding forth, began to pay dividends. The Board of Trustees was on the brink of dropping poor old Bill for good. He was already in the 'special advisor' limbo, and his almost magically producing the real artifacts safe and sound hadn't done him much good at all it seemed. Too much subterfuge and confusion. Too many fires; too many robberies. So the cards must be played very circumspectly. Professional life and social death were on the table.

The atmosphere around this particular table was decidedly uncomfortable, while eyes were failing to meet in very obvious ways. It's not often that somebody who is almost *persona non grata* brazenly shows up for bridge as if nothing had happened, stares the other three boldly in the eye, and cuts the cards with the practiced hand of a steamboat sharper. Bold as brass. That's the navy way!

'All right, let's go! Ready to have yer clocks cleaned?'

Normally, the chatter would go in waves as the cards were shuffled, dealt and fanned out. It would rise during the mechanical action of dealing and fall off completely during periods of bidding, concentration and play. It followed a sawtooth wave pattern. On this occasion the talk was stilted and a cold cloud hung over the table.

Warning, thought Doris, bridge can get icy.

But as the tricks were taken one by one the talk became freer, although steered resolutely away from any reference to the museum. It was all gossip of the most trivial and fatuous kind—and all the more hurtful for its absent recipients in consequence—a sort of empty point scoring that made the card game look quite trivial. Now there was a fevered, frenetic quality to the chatter, underscoring the social embarrassment of the occasion. One talked in order not to think. The chatter came around to newspapers.

'Well, we always take *The Townsperson*. We know Worton very well, of course.'

Worton was a columnist with exceedingly right wing, militant Christian views, combining these with a conspicuous lack of analytical attributes. He was an ardent supporter of American military aggression, and considered his government's stands on international politics, gay rights and abortion to be little short of cowardice.

'Ye-e-ss, good journalism is such a comfort, isn't it?'

'Must be so-o-o wonderful to write so-o-o well.'

Doris saw an opening and swooped like a barn owl to a crunchy field mouse.

'Well, we're very good friends with Randall, of course.'

This was a barefaced lie, and she only hoped she would get away with it. Randall was a muckraking columnist for the other newspaper in town, the one that claimed to be the people's voice. It was smaller in size and showed tits. She actually despised this more than all other forms of journalism. Mention of this particular rag in the present company was the breath of bowels during a church service.

'Always on the lookout for scandal, is Randall!'

The chatter died down for a hand or so. Doris was really being quite *gauche* tonight. Perhaps her husband's upcoming fall from grace was too much, poor dear? Still, what delicious material for our next little soirée! After a few more cards had fallen, the prattle rose again to its former level. Now they were on to fur coats.

'Ooh, yes, that Melanie LaNièce! It was so-o-o obviously fake fur, but she told me it was mink!'

'Isn't it awful to try fooling people like that?'

'Specially when it's so obvious!'

'Well, you know, just between us,' said one of the others in a ridiculous fake whisper, eyes scanning the four corners of the room as if seeking phantom video eavesdroppers, 'her husband's not doing as well as she makes out. In fact, he's looking at... *bankruptcy.*'

This was the second barefaced lie of the evening. In fact he was on a very stable financial footing.

'That's still no reason to pretend you've got a mink when you haven't! Hah!'

'Yes,' observed Doris, sensing her moment and joining the conversation for only the second time. She now saw how the cards could be made to fall; the ones in her hand were crap by comparison.

'It's the worst kind of trickery, trying to convince somebody that something is what it isn't.'

It took a while for this loaded pronouncement to filter into their heads. She was obviously alluding to the museum. There was a new tension in the play. The chatter abated. The cards now passed around in glacial silence. The deals flopped down; bidding was in monotones. The tricks came and went.

'It would be immoral,' Doris observed dryly a short time later, 'to conceal the truth from anybody.'

Again the play resumed in tense silence, only a murmuring over bids and points.

'Take my husband,' observed Doris again into the vacuum. 'Very moral man. He inherited a whole museum full of fakes.'

Another hand in tense silence. Bridge was getting very icy.

'Hard not to come clean. Spill the beans. Said so to Randall only the other day.'

Riffle and flap of cards.

'But as the *director* his lips would be sealed, of course.'

Silence.

'Lucky, really. I mean, for the reputation of the museum...'

On Monday morning Doris barged into Mutcer's temporary lair in Building Two. He had camped out after the fire in a storage room. No posters adorned the bare walls, and it all looked very temporary and makeshift. It was deeply offensive to Doris to penetrate so far into enemy territory, and the defensive miasma that the enemy put up reminded her of chemical warfare. Still, she was here, and she had a job to do.

'What are you doing in here? Security should have stopped you!'

'He let me in. Knowing stuff about people opens doors.'

'Get out! Get out!'

'Not a hope,' she replied with a smile. No subtleties this time. She ran the cannon out and launched in. 'So, how did you enjoy burning a museum down?'

Mutcer wasn't having any of it. He had regained some of his confidence since his public humiliation and now he was actually hatching schemes to have Mrs Ironside-Anker hauled into court. He had met the day before with his attorney, Mr Aaron Dovetail, of Mortise, Tenon, Dovetail and McDowell, Attorneys at Law. Mr Dovetail had advised him that, given witnesses who would come forward, he certainly had a case. So he was feeling full of piss and vinegar and wasn't going to sit down and take anything. (In fact, since the blazing hip flask incident, he was having trouble taking anything sitting down.) He went straight in to parry the attack.

'Don't you talk to me like that! And how dare you accuse me of such a heinous crime! I'll sue you for all this!'

'Where's your copy of Lucien Limace's fire report?' she shot back.

He was caught off guard. What was this? He didn't even know she knew of the existence of Limace's report, let alone that it might be faked. Recovering quickly, he yelled:

'It's none of your business! Get out of here! Out!'

'It *is* my business! Because I'll bet it's not signed! How much do you wanna bet there's no signature on it?'

Goaded, he swung round angrily to his filing cabinet, riffled through the contents, and withdrew a cream-coloured folder. Out came the report.

'There! Course it's signed!' He shoved the copy into her face.

She wrinkled her nose, sniffing.

'See?' he crowed. 'What the hell are you trying to prove?'

'Nothing,' she replied sweetly. 'Nothing at all. The presence or absence of a signature was just a ruse. Nothing at all, except that of all the offices, galleries, and rooms in the entire east wing, only the contents of yours seem to have been saved from the fire. Why, this folder doesn't even smell slightly smoky. Lucky you rescued it *before* the blaze! Got crystal balls, have you?'

'I don't have to listen to this! You have nothing against me! You get out of here! I'll call security!'

'Call him. Think he'll come?' She paused, drilling him with her eyes. 'Well, smoky smell, my friend. What of it?'

His face showed that he had realized his fundamental error. He wasn't about to buckle, but this sideswipe had softened him up. Time for Doris to fire the broadside before he could reply.

'Okay, let's cut the bullshit you stupid little squirt! I'm not here to listen to you driveling. I'm here to give you instructions.'

'I don't take instructions!' he bounced back. 'I take legal action! I will not be publicly humiliated, I will not be accused of anything, and I will have my day in court! You'll see!'

'You *will* take instructions you smelly piece of offal, and I'll tell you why.'

'You're not telling me anything! Get out of here! If you think you can push me around...'

He stood up and made to come around the desk.

'Yes, I think I bloody well can! See this?'

And she withdrew a tape cassette from her handbag and waved it in his face.

'You didn't know Mr Anker was wired for sound when you threatened him, did you? Eh? That little hearing aid? You fucking dolt! A transceiver my friend, and you are *recorded*.'

Mutcer turned white and then red by turns. He fell back into his chair. His hands began to shake, and he sought and applied his little flask without thinking. Like a trapped animal, he cowered and seemed actually to shrink.

'Yes,' she continued smoothly, 'I could shop you to the cops right now.'

'Whu... whu... you...' he bubbled.

'But I might not... Oh, no. I think I'll just give you another damned good thrashing instead.'

This was a strategic error, but only a small one. She had the distinct impression that this threat had stimulated some horrible pleasure centre in her victim, and that was the last thing she wanted.

She made a pretence of thinking deeply, while Rourke Mutcer cowered in front of her.

'No, on second thoughts, I think the law is the answer.'

She turned as if to leave the room.

The gambit worked. Mutcer broke.

'No, no, no! Come back! What do you want? What do you want?'

'What do I want?' she answered slowly and quietly. 'What do I *want?* Your good behaviour. That's what I want. Your absolute and unequivocal promise that you will never aspire to my husband's job.

Your assurance that from now on you will be a model patient in this lunatic asylum they call a museum. And I will be watching you in ways you can never even dream of. I have the ear of God Almighty in the shape of the Board of Trustees. And information that the cops would find very interesting. One little deviation from the path I set for you, and you are finished. Do you understand me? *Well, do you?'*

He nodded that he understood. He was beyond speech. He sat at his desk unmoving.

'I am watching you. And I can grind you to powder under my heel, you piece of insufferable garbage!'

She scooped up the incriminating file folder from the desk, tucked it under her arm, and left the room. Before passing through the door she returned the blank, unused cassette nonchalantly to her purse.

Once out of the building and across the parking lot she let down her control and began to shake. What a gamble! God, what a gamble! As she sat behind the wheel of her car, she scarcely believed she'd had the nerve to pull it off. As she calmed down and the trembling lessened, a sense of elation rose within her. God, it was good to push that little bastard around! Better not get to like it too much... Soon she was ready to start the engine and pull out of the parking lot. She almost wished she had a little flask.

Easel did not fare as well as Mutcer (if being condemned to suck-hole around Anker for the rest of your career could be called faring well). The evening of the museum dinner turned out to be Easel's last as a free man for some time. An executive assistant at the museum, whose purse had been stolen some weeks earlier, received an anonymous phone call on Saturday morning. The caller told her in great detail exactly where her purse could be found. The caller advised her against direct action and suggested the police. She went straight to the nearest police station and reported the call.

The chief of police, Sergeant Delios, and two constables appeared at Building Four later that morning with a search warrant. Easel had dragged himself into the lab even though he should have stayed at home. He had a huge lump on the back of his head, and Big Jim and the Twins were twice their normal size, and dark blue. Pissing was a nightmare. His mood was foul.

Sure enough, once the police had flashed their search warrant and removed a ceiling tile above Easel's desk, they were able to retrieve a cache of small, valuable articles and personal effects that had been reported missing by staff, or had been stolen from the museum's collections. Among these was the executive assistant's purse. More significantly, the hoard included the solid gold Japanese statuette.

Easel's claim that he had no idea how they had 'gotten' there cut no mustard with the cops. Especially when they had first removed a cardboard file box containing copious notes, memos and transcripts of conversations and phone calls made by staff, all neatly arranged by name. The investigators were not concerned with the content of this sleazy material, but it was excellent evidence for the fact that Easel knew of the hiding place, and used it frequently.

Realizing that somebody was framing him—and having a damned good idea who—Easel should have maintained that famous icy control. But being in pulsating blue/black pain, and caught totally by surprise with his hidden box of notes in front of him, he wasn't exactly in full control of his emotions. So, when they tried to read him his rights the red curtain came down again; he blew up. It certainly didn't help his case when he struggled and punched and clawed and even used his teeth on them. One of the constables needed rabies shots, and Delios nursed bruises and cuts that wouldn't heal for weeks.

No one posted bail for Easel. As soon as the truth about him was out—and people earnestly wanted to believe that this *was* the truth, and most hugged themselves with glee when they heard of it—all those he had charmed, won over, manipulated, cajoled or threatened deserted him. Once the meaty paw of the law was fastened to his collar their allegiances or fears evaporated. So, he languished in the slammer awaiting trial.

The activists were never caught, or even seen again. They could have been hunted down by the police and charged for a whole slew of infractions. The ringleaders, at least, were on police files in great detail, and it would have been simplicity itself to trace the rental of the truck back to them. It might even have been possible to blame the fire on them, with the circumstantial evidence alone. However, the museum chose not to press any charges. This pissed off the chief of police mightily. But it was mooted among the Board of Trustees that the less information the general public had on the exact nature of that collection, and of the somewhat lax security services at the museum, the better. Furthermore, having the artifacts—the real ones—back safely in the museum's care made the rest unimportant.

John Indoda Enhle never would say what had happened after

179

that nighttime chase, when he went roaring down deserted side streets in pursuit of the activists, but there was always a grim twinkle in his eye when the subject was raised. It had been a defining experience for him.

He now met often with the museum staff on both formal and informal occasions. His closer association with the museum—and the museum's recognition that he was more than just a useful native tool—made for an enduring and mutually rewarding relationship.

He was involved as a consultant in identifying and checking the newly recovered Treaty Bluff artifacts, and it was he who got those goddamned string players banished for good from all museum functions. From now on, you want to celebrate the stuff my people made, you have drummers and dancers!

But he could never stop smiling, and nobody knew why.

Lucian Limace decided to slide quietly into retirement without even needing to be coerced, and it is hardly necessary to report that he found the difference between retirement and his job at the museum imperceptible. So, when it came time to topple him out of the chief's chair, Limace was replaced—initially in an acting capacity—by a quite young man, scarcely over thirty. He hadn't been at the museum long before this surprise promotion, and some argued that he didn't have the experience for the job. However, he had a tremendous resumé, and since the fire and thefts he had taken the initiative in proposing new guard routines and recommending the purchase of advanced security equipment, and had made himself very useful in many other ways. All this over the head of Lucien Limace, who not only seemed powerless to curb him, but actually appeared to encourage his activities.

When the permanent job was advertised the new guard's name naturally came forward. He was supported almost one hundred percent by the other guards, mostly because he had made sure to treat them with respect and cut them a bit of slack. They had much to hide—especially the night shift men—and he cleverly ran interference for them. None of the older men resented the promotion anyway; they were quite content where they were and, being mostly ex-servicemen, they knew their position and knew also that elevated rank doesn't always bring peace of mind. The new man actually worked out very well and soon had museum security running with an efficiency unheard of in past years.

Mrs Straw and the Board of Trustees appeared to be favourably impressed with Bill Anker's conduct and demeanour from the time of the cataclysmic museum dinner onward. The Board had convened soon after the dinner and having studied further evidence, had decided to rescind his demotion to Special Advisor. Mrs Straw had met with him a week later to give him the good news. This sounded all very judicial and forgiving, but that was just the spin she put on it. After the little bridge evening, the Board had become shit scared that the whole mess would become public, especially if a director was demoted or sacked and the truth got out. This was one of those plaster-over-the-cracks jobs that government bodies are so skilled at.

So, Bill Anker's humiliation was reversed and erased almost before it had really begun. In spite of its politically astute decision, the Board had noticed, as had so many others, that Anker appeared remarkably changed in behaviour. He was more assertive, more organized and less prone to fits of dithering vacillation. Not one person suspected the beneficial effects of a program of radio control.

Stephanie Chang took over as acting chief of conservation and it looked to become permanent as soon as a staffing competition could be held, and the results tipped in favour of the incumbent. They wouldn't make the Easel mistake a second time. The first two months would prove to be a trial by fire, and she would sometimes wish she had never taken it on. A huge effort would have to be expended, and very diplomatically, in divesting the Conservation Department of its intricately ramified empire of influence, and getting its fingers gently but firmly out of other people's pies. In addition, the entire database of conservation treatment and reproductions would need to be reviewed and revised.

Then there were the conservators. They would have to be weaned away from their addiction to measuring, surveying and bean counting, and brought back to the tangible reality of artifacts, materials and treatment techniques. But there was also the social/psychological problem of reintegrating them into a museum workforce that had pretty well washed its hands of them. But the conservation staff were ordinary decent people, and once the vicious C-clamp of repression was removed from their professional lives, they flowered dramatically in harmony with the season. And the other museum staff, sensing the transformation, made room for them at the communal table.

The Carpenter made a reappearance as the March snow was receding, and warm spring was beckoning. The Carpenter's name, coincidentally, was Brian. He wasn't such a bad guy after all, and Stephanie felt awful when she remembered how she had taken Easel's word on the man, even against her better judgement. Even at the age of 30 she found she had some learning and some growing up to do. She was now making amends. It wasn't hard to find him a contract for treating some of the backlog of artifacts. He was sensitive and very skilled, and it wasn't long before he cottoned on to the museum's documentation techniques. He was also a gifted organizer. Once he was on permanent staff it might be possible for him to pick up some academic training, and get paper qualifications. From carpentry to conservation.

All in all, this Brian seemed to be working out much better than the last one...

The Carpenter himself decided to ride this wave of good fortune for as long as it stayed under him, because when you-know-who was a free man again he was as good as dead.

The enquiries of the Police on the causes of the fire had been inconclusive. In their report it was necessary to state that the fire in the old museum had been started by a person or persons unknown, and although they had their suspicions, that was all they were. The chief of police was deeply pissed off for quite a while about this as well. It was a tangled mess: he had an obvious culprit, the obvious culprit was equally obviously innocent, he had a good idea who might be guilty, but he didn't have a shred of evidence that would stand up in court, and to top it off the lot of them were bloody loonies. The side of his finger was chewed raw. The files stayed open. And Sergeant Delios was totally sick of being hauled down to the cafeteria almost daily, and being forced to drink dreadful drafts of spine-shuddering coffee while listening to interminable, circular theories and scenarios.

On a positive note, at least the thief who had plagued the museum for so long was safely behind bars awaiting trial. Seeing justice done so convincingly was one of those positive affirmations that made being a cop so worthwhile.

The case against Woodrow Wilson Easel eventually went before the courts. The diplomatic fuss over the gold statuette had ensured a high profile. This was not simply part of a series of petty thefts; it was robbery with international repercussions, and it soon became a juicy media event.

The prosecution brought forward four witnesses. The first was the young security guard who had been on duty the day of the theft. He revealed the fact that Easel had entered the building that afternoon around 3:00. No, there was no record of Easel's presence in the building; he hadn't signed in. When asked why he didn't accost him at the door he stated that, because he was a museum employee of long-standing, it was unnecessary. The guard categorically denied Easel's version of events; he denied speaking with him, and also denied making any phone call to him. It was touch-and-go, but he didn't crack. His friendship with the Carpenter had come at a heavy emotional price. When cross examined about the disposition of the display case at the end of his shift, he could not unequivocally state if the gold statuette was still there or not. After the demonstration and riot, things were just too chaotic.

The second witness was the overnight security guard, and he had a miserable time of it because it was clear that he had not checked the displays in detail all night. He bent under examination, but didn't spill the beans. The boozing in the loading bay would remain a secret. Such was their solidarity.

The third witness, the executive assistant who had been contacted by phone, repeated the material contained in her statement to the police, but could add nothing further. No, she could not identify the voice of her informant.

The prosecution had also brought forward video evidence. A surveillance camera had caught Easel briefly in the vicinity of the display case and, most significantly, using the special screwdriver required for access. This he had admitted, but when his version of the story came out in court, the disbelief on most faces was clearly writ. Then, the next sequence of the video—on the camera's next scan—showed the display case standing empty, with the lid beside it on the floor.

Even more damning than the video was the fact that Easel's fingerprints, and nobody else's, were all over the gold statuette. His counsel argued that the fingerprints could easily have got onto the piece at the time of installation, but this is where the fourth prosecution witness came in.

The same carpenter whom Easel had sacked without notice had been contacted by the police during their sweep for witnesses to the events surrounding the installation and display of *Gold and Gems*. Under questioning, he swore that Easel had used white cotton gloves the whole time during the display installation. It was absolutely inconceivable, he argued, for a conservator of such reputation to handle an object in any other way. Oh, the repercussions of forgetting to put on the little white gloves!

This testimony caused such an outburst of spleen from the defendant that the court had to be adjourned for a day. Indeed, throughout the whole trial Easel's defence was unfortunately marred by irrational outbursts, accusations of framing, and lurid threats to get even. Several times during the proceedings the judge mooted whether it might be advisable to send the defendant for psychiatric evaluation as the trial was being disturbed and extended considerably, but his attorney, Mr Sean Phillips of Robertson, Phillips, Allen and Slothead, managed to stave this off.

Mr Phillips was unable to control the outbursts at all, though, and he was thoroughly sick of his client. He had even considered slipping a cap of Valium into his morning gruel—or whatever it was they fed felons in the holding cells—as a last resort. In desperation, and in the absence of any evidence that might indicate that his client was not guilty, Phillips tried to find character witnesses. Before the museum dinner he might have counted on Stephanie Chang and the other conservators, but not now. Seeing which side their bread was buttered on, nobody was interested.

Once he saw which side his own bread had been margarined on, Easel lost control spectacularly, right there in the dock, and amid vicious swearing of vengeance and kicking and clawing, he was taken away. He would never be the same again. Something in him was permanently extinguished that day, and he became a hollow shell.

Phillips was almost certain he could have got his client off—the evidence was circumstantial at best, and the witnesses suspicious— if only he had been able to control the outbursts of temper. On second thoughts, maybe he should have agreed with the judge and ordered that psychiatric evaluation…

As it was, the idiot had just about condemned himself.

So, Easel was screwed, and an innocent man went to the slammer.

Crocodile tears anybody?

CHAPTER TWENTY-ONE

B ill Anker was surrounded by sycophantic museum officials, Mrs Straw, members of the Board, and the minister of Culture and Professional Sport, among the surveyor's stakes and grid lines of the new museum, sipping a tall glass of Caves Barquelet. Caterers had set up tables covered by an awning and laid out a range of wines, soft drinks, and delectable munchies. The influence of the Chair of the Board was evident in the selection, quality and quantity of the offerings.

On this flat piece of land beside the river would rise the edifice Bill had hoped for and dreamed of for so long. It was now some months after the disastrous and triumphant museum dinner and the events that had preceded it. Spring was in full flush; the weather was warm and dry and his mood mirrored the climate. Two lines from Shakespeare rippled into his thoughts:

Now is the winter of our discontent,
Made glorious summer by this scum of Pork

Things happened amazingly quickly after the New Year. An extremely wealthy, and so far, anonymous, benefactor had come forward with a pledge. He was somebody with a large amount of money; an almost obscenely large amount of money. Seeing this largesse, and the opportunity to get a new museum at half price, the government had come forward with a pledge of matching funds. Lord knows what political contrails had interwoven high up in the stratosphere of power, but who cared? The results were what counted. For a government organization, the speed of progress had been as breathtaking as it was unprecedented.

Practically before he knew it, Bill Anker, his building committee, and selected members of the Board had been presented with three competition proposals; cardboard and plastic miniatures of extraordinary detail and intricacy, which would become museum pieces in their own right. He did not want an ostentatious building that looked like a standing ovation for its architect. He was clear on this. He did not want a building that shoved itself in your face and said: 'Look at me. Isn't my architect clever?' No sinuous lines, no stainless-steel drums like piles of battered garbage cans, no crystal palaces. Bill Anker wanted a building that stood aside metaphorically, and doffed its hat to the visitors. He wanted a building that would defer to its contents, and there are not many top-of-the-line architects who are prepared to lower themselves to such servitude. He was adamant, and the new Bill Anker got his way.

Two offerings were rejected by the combined committee; works of art they undoubtedly were, and material for sunset scenes on postcards most certainly, but not worthy containers for museum pieces. They would squabble too much with their contents. The third, however, was presented by a relatively young local architect who had yet to make a name for herself. New to the profession as she was—she had only a few minor civic buildings to her credit—she was not yet endowed with that arrogance that comes with the success of great projects. Her submission was conservative, attractive and unassuming, and exactly what Anker was after. Also, because it was a no-frills sort of design, it was very much more economical than the other two submissions. This meant more money for the details of infrastructure so often lacking in museums designed by Architects with a capital A.

Models had progressed to drawings in a few short months and now here in the ground, lit and shadowed by the sloping afternoon sun, were the stakes and strings to show where the building would be. Here in front of Bill was the grand hall, over there the curatorial wing, and to this side the amalgamated and consolidated storage rooms and workshops where, finally, he could have all his people under one roof!

Everything else had worked out wonderfully as well. Easel a threat no more, Mutcer well under control, and seething as his dreams slipped away. A whole new universe of opportunity was opening before Anker, and the dread engendered by having to show up at work every day had ceased. A new, blossoming and fertile world surrounded him and Doris, his dear wife. He had never felt so self-confident, so in control. And it wasn't just the booze.

Now it was time for the ritual sod-turning where the congregation would assemble round the minister of Culture and Professional Sport as he wielded the ceremonial shovel, silver-plated, engraved, and one-use disposable. A single thrust, a shovelful of soil thrown aside, and that was enough work for him for one day. The crowd clapped and cheered.

Bill spotted John Indoda Enhle, and started to work his way over to him, glass in hand. Indoda Enhle was partaking of the wine and munchies, and making a supreme and excruciating effort to hide his mirth. Previously, the secret he had held in for so long had been an onus; a responsibility, and a nagging worry. Something he would rather not have been privy to. But after the events of the last few months the humour became inescapable.

When you looked hard at it, life was so deeply and richly ironic. It all came of these newcomers taking things so seriously. All this pandemonium around the museum came from their insistence on authenticity. That was it! The idea of living an authentic life. They had to have the real thing, didn't they? And they would lie and steal and cheat and burn buildings down for it. And now they were so pleased with themselves; slugging down their wine, banging each other on the back, and anticipating the great day when the Treaty Bluff collection would be displayed for all the world in opulent surroundings fit to show off its excellence. He smiled; something he had been doing a hell of a lot just recently.

What was it his old Dad had said? Dad, the ultimate trickster. Oh, yes. He could remember it almost word for word. He must have been about 11 or 12 years old. He had sat as close to the cast iron stove as he could because it was cold and damp that night. There were always lots of logs, and it was his young job to keep to stove stoked. Quite a few people were packed into the room. Dad was fond of lighting a cigarette of an evening, shaking his match out in that characteristic loose-wristed way, and yarning about this and that; whatever came into his head. John received most of his real education this way. Elementary school at Treaty Bluff in those days was a waste of time really. Not too many kids had much time for the white man's spin on the history of their own land, and they weren't all that big on memorizing tables of so-called facts either. No, for lots like him they learned about the world and life and their place around the stoves, along the trap lines, and in the boats out fishing. It was only later that school, Western style, had come to mean anything useful to him.

Yes, he recalled the old man's words that night almost exactly.

'Back in my father's time; your granddaddy—this would be, oh 1912, 1913 maybe—the white museum people and whatnot came through here collecting stuff. Stealing really; we had no say in the matter and they had their laws on their side. Our people; we couldn't do this, we couldn't do that, we couldn't do nothing. If you was a local in those days you shut up and did what you were told. Hasn't changed much neither. Jeez, we were off our land, couldn't hunt, couldn't fish, couldn't do *shit!*

'Anyways, they leave and head further west. South too. Over rivers and far away. Year or so later they come back again with crates and boxes of stuff. All the gear they'd lifted from our people with their crazy laws from hundreds of miles around, and they're just going to leave it all here in Treaty Bluff until they can ship it east. Then the war comes in Europe, eh? Their attention's elsewhere, ain't it? And here's this collection of stuff, just sittin' in boxes doing nothing.

'Well, your granddaddy and some of the other elders, they got together to think what to do. They made a circle in our way and they thought and they talked and they smoked. It was a golden opportunity. It didn't take long to decide, neither. Know what they did? They took every single goddam piece out of every single goddam box and crate, and they got wood and leather and paint and stuff, and they took their tools, and they copied 'em! Every one!

'There were some good carvers around then. (There still were, of course, John's kid brother James included.) They didn't have to copy them real accurate 'cos there was no one checking anyways. But, hell, they even tied pissy little labels on 'em! Well, they weren't doing much else with their time in those days. What they put back in the boxes was the copies!'

Triple take.

'And the originals? Well, that's the funniest bit of all. They had everything about them written up all nice and neat in big notebooks, and our people had plenty of time on their hands. Shouldn'ta taught us how to read at them schools!' They all laughed uproariously at that. 'Anyhow, they gave 'em all back. Far and wide. Every damned one of them! Took months—near on a year—but if you're going to do a job, you got to do it right. Ain't that so?'

And they had all roared with laughter again together around the stove.

'So, things went the right way for us that time,' his father had said when the laughter had finally died down. 'And things went the wrong way for the museum guys. Lesson for life, my boy. Some things go the right way, and some things go the wrong way. But you gotta push!'

Bill Anker, all aglow, glass in hand, a smile on his innocent face, had been waylaid by well-wishers continuously before finally making his way around to where John Indoda Enhle stood contemplating the day's doings and running history through his mind.

'Well, things really have gone the right way!'

Indoda Enhle exploded. His cheeks puffed out, his face reddened, and white wine spurted. The coughing fit lasted a good minute and left him helpless, breathless, and not a little embarrassed.

'Sorry,' he gasped, as he mopped his face with a tissue and regained a little composure. 'Something must have gone the wrong way.'

But he had developed a proprietary glow toward the museum, and had become one of its major supporters in high political places. Unknown to any of that organization's administrators, he had been consulted extensively during the winter by an extremely well-heeled and anonymous individual on the viability of this new museum plan. His say-so had tipped the balance. He and Daddy, the Admiral, had enjoyed a very fruitful collaboration.

So, while he kept his mouth shut on the authenticity of the Treaty Bluff collection, he saw that there was actually some very good stuff in the museum, mostly in the storage collections that the public never saw. Some legitimately acquired pieces would be good to display; others might need to go back where they rightfully belonged. He would see to it that things were different in the new museum.

One piece in the Treaty Bluff collection, above all others, intrigued him, though: the mask of N'ufnīvah, the Hare. The trickster. The more he thought about what he had found, the less he really understood. There was the 'original,' and then there was the copy. It subsequently turned out that both were false. The one the police had examined as evidence was synthetic, as was the one that bowled toward him down the table that fateful evening.

There *was* no original.

Where the original had gone was anybody's guess, and it was probably somebody's dark secret. Mr Kaliman had made them both; they were definitely made of resin and fiberglass. He knew this at first hand because he had been contracted by the museum to examine all the pieces for authenticity not long after their recovery. So, how was it then, that when he reexamined the Hare just recently it proved to be made of wood? Not new wood; old, well worn, well used, historic wood. And, you know, he would swear that, out of the corner of his eye, just as he turned away, it had winked at him.

Nah...

The newly self-confident director of the finest collection of WeWho crafts in the country left Indoda Enhle after a few congratulatory exchanges, and continued on his rounds. He guzzled down his plonk and swiped another glass from a passing tray. This was the life! It was just drinking and small talk now until going home time.

Eventually Doris Ironside-Anker sailed up to him, let fall her mains'ls and hove to nicely. She was on the wave crest of her existence in interlocking ways. The museum director kit that she had been assembling for a decade was turning out to be a success, and within her she had felt the first small stirrings of a little golden goddess. They knew it was a girl; no sense in taking chances at her age. Their very own Nereid! Galatea sounded quite nice, or perhaps Arethusa? And soon it would be time to tell Bill about Daddy's 'anonymous' role in all of this.

'Time we were leaving for home, my dear,' she said in a passionate whisper, gripping him above the elbow. It's amazing what happiness, contentedness, and fulfillment will do. And the odd gin and tonic.

Fireworks.

EPILOGUE

John Indoda Enhle had heard a 'thunk' and had seen a glint of light when the minister had shoved the ceremonial silver-plated spade into the ground, but it hadn't really registered. As the afternoon wore on, though, he thought more about it, and it intrigued him. He decided to hang around, and it was with some impatience that he watched the last stragglers, eyeing the bottles and glasses reflectively, and finally wending their way. Now the site was almost empty. The caterers were picking up plastic wine glasses and packing tables and tablecloths. A waiter in short tailcoat and cravat was recorking half-finished bottles and putting them into a crate; he and his buddies should have a good time tonight.

Sunlight slanted orange and threw blades of grass into high relief. The site of the sod turning, a little way over from the refreshments, was deserted. Indoda Enhle wandered nonchalantly over there, and glancing once over each shoulder to ensure that he wasn't observed, crouched down to examine the hole the spade had carved into the soft soil. The glint of light he had seen was a flint arrowhead that had fortuitously caught the sun. And the 'thunk' was a femur.

'Hmm,' thought the arts representative of the We Who Were Here First as he stroked the ancient, ochre-stained bone.

'New museum? Here? On this sacred land? Well, I guess we've come this far, so... let's see how this can be done...

'*But just look who'll be calling the shots!*'

www.ingramcontent.com/pod-product-compliance
Lightning Source LLC
LaVergne TN
LVHW041251080426
835510LV00009B/682